w to Use
s Book

O SYMBOLS

Map reference to the accompanying fold-out map

Address

Telephone number

Opening/closing times

Restaurant or café

Nearest rail station

Nearest Metro (subway) station

Nearest bus route

Nearest riverboat or ferry stop

Facilities for visitors with disabilities

? Other practical information

▷ Further information

ℹ Tourist information

✋ Admission charges: Expensive (over €6), Moderate (€3–6) and Inexpensive (€3 or less)

★ Major Sight   ★ Minor Sight

👣 Walks

🚌 Excursions

🛍 Shops

🎵 Entertainment and Nightlife

🍴 Restaurants

s guide is divided into four sections

ssential Milan: an introduction to the city and tips on king the most of your stay.

ilan by Area: We've broken the city into five areas, and ommended the best sights, shops, entertainment venues, ntlife and restaurants in each one. Suggested walks help you explore on foot.

here to Stay: the best hotels, whether you're looking for ury, budget or something in between.

eed to Know: the info you need to make your trip run oothly, including getting about by public transport, weather , emergency phone numbers and useful websites.

vigation In the Milan by Area chapter, we've given each area wn tint, which is also used on the locator maps throughout book and the map on the inside front cover.

ps The fold-out map accompanying this book is a comprehen-e street plan of Milan. The grid on this fold-out map is the ne as the grid on the locator maps within the book. We've en grid references within the book for each sight and listing.

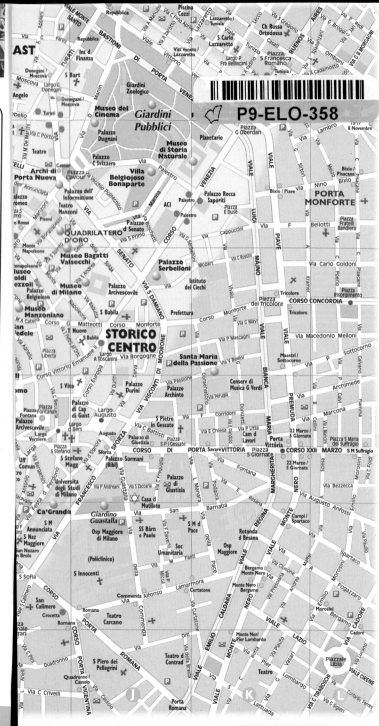

P9-ELO-358

Fodor's

Milan's
25Best

by Jackie Staddon and Hilary West

Fodor's Travel Publications
New York • Toronto
London • Sydney • Auckland
www.fodors.com

This
• Es
mal
• M
reco
nigl
to e
• W
luxu
• N
sm
tips

Na
its
the

Ma
siv
sa
giv

Contents

Introducing Milan

There's an old adage, 'Milan l'è Milan'—Milan is just Milan. And though the city may seem to lack the charm of other Italian cities, if you scratch beneath the surface you will find this is a city of contrasts and hidden depths, with its own unique personality.

Milan's reputation is one of commercialism driven by market forces, and indeed it is the powerhouse of Italy's economy. But this city is not just about commercialism. Despite the Milanese modern approach to business and their trendy get-up-and-go ways, the traditional Italian lifestyle has not been totally rejected.

Milan has some of the finest churches in Italy and numerous *palazzi*, proud reminders of the city's aristocratic past. The many well-run museums offer a glimpse into the city's artistic and historic heritage. There is fantastic shopping at every level, from chic designer stores to street markets. And the style doesn't stop with fashion; even the humblest delicatessens have a certain flair.

Just beyond the *centro storico* there are other districts with a totally different feel, like the Navigli, where renovation is rejuvenating the area. You will also discover pretty parks and hidden gardens that act as tranquil oases from the hustle and bustle.

While it does have a lot of traffic and rush hour congestion, the city is a comfortable place to live and exudes a sense of well being—and, unlike some other Italian cities, the Milanese don't make excessive use of their car horns. Public transportation is excellent: efficient, clean and reasonably priced. The Milanese are happy in their own skin, unruffled and confident—busy, yes, but they always find time to be sociable.

Milan may not have the beauty of Florence, the grandeur of Rome or the romance of Venice, but it does have something very appealing all of its own.

Facts + Figures

- Area of city: 181.7sq km (70sq miles)
- Population: 1.3 million (Greater Milan: 4 million) in 2005
- The Duomo is the third-largest church in the world
- Trade fairs in Milan draw over 4 million visitors per year

MILAN FOR FREE

There are many free museums in Milan and churches do not charge for entry, although there may be a small fee to see a specific painting. Parco Sempione is free to wander but its various attractions may carry a fee. Exploring the canal district and the old artist quarter of Brera or window-shopping in the designer streets won't cost anything either—that's if you can resist.

MILAN'S SKYSCRAPERS

The most famous of these is the Edificio Pirelli, familiarly known as Big Pirelli, which remains one of the symbols of Milan. Designed by Gio Ponti and Pier Luigi Nervi—completed in 1960—it is the tallest at 127m (417ft). This is followed closely by the Milan skyscraper at 114m (374ft), the Galfa building at 104m (341ft) and the Velasca Tower at 99m (325ft).

FASHION SHOWS

Milan was first catapulted into the limelight as Europe's fashion capital in 1971, when Italy's largest international fashion show was moved here from Florence. Today, the autumn and winter collections of leading designers grace the catwalks at the Fiera de Milano in early March, while the spring and summer collections take the stage in October.

A Short Stay in Milan

DAY 1

Morning Beat the crowds and start your day around 8.30 at the **Pinacoteca di Brera** (▷ 27), which has the best art collection in the city.

Mid-morning Just a short walk south is **Teatro alla Scala** (▷ 52); take a peek inside this famous opera house as you pass by. Stroll through **Galleria Vittorio Emanuele II** (▷ 48), taking in a few shops along the way. Stop for a coffee break at **Zucca** (▷ 60) and watch the world go by while admiring the **Duomo** (▷ 46–47) laid out before you. Visit the Duomo and, on a fine day, scale the 165 steps for an unbeatable view of the city.

Lunch Seek out one of the tempting eateries in or around Piazza Duomo; try **Dai Damm** (▷ 59) on Via Torino or perhaps **Charleston** (▷ 59) in Piazza del Liberty, or head up Corso Vittorio Emanuele II, where there are several more options.

Afternoon If you continue along Corso Vittorio Emanuele II to Via Montenapoleone and go north, you will find yourself in the **Quadrilatero d'Oro** (▷ 28–29). Spend the rest of the afternoon exploring this network of pretty streets known as the Golden Quad—Milan's sensational shopping area—but go easy on your credit card. In the middle of the afternoon, try to work your way toward **Cova** (▷ 39), where you can rest your weary feet while you have a coffee and mouthwatering cake.

Dinner From the top end of Montenapoleone, it's only a short walk west to the **Brera district** (▷ 74). Join in 'happy hour' at one of the trendy bars and then have a unique dining experience at **Orient Express** (▷ 78).

Evening After dinner wander around the winding medieval streets of this attractive area, soaking up the lively atmosphere.

DAY 2

Morning Reserve tickets well in advance to admire da Vinci's *Last Supper* first thing in the morning at **Santa Maria delle Grazie** (▷ 72–73). If you don't have tickets, check out the beautiful church and its cloisters instead.

Mid-morning Walk a little farther on down Corso Magenta to **Biffi** (▷ 78) for a quick pit-stop before heading north to **Parco Sempione** (▷ 70). Enter the park on the west side, pass the Palazzo dell'Arte and for a great view take the elevator to the top of the Torre Branca. Spend some time rambling among the lakes, modern sculptures and monuments.

Lunch There are several cafés in the park where you can have lunch or, if the weather is fine, take a picnic lunch to eat on the grass.

Afternoon Head toward the northeast perimeter of the park and pay a visit to the **Acquario** (▷ 74). Leave this underwater world behind and follow the path round to the clocktower at the front of Castello Sforzesco.

Mid-afternoon Wander down the wide, walkable Via Dante, packed with café options for a coffee break. Retrace your steps back to **Castello Sforzesco** (▷ 66–67) and go inside the massive fortress for a look around. If you have time, visit one of the Castello's interesting museums or relax in the courtyard gardens.

Dinner Take the metro from Cadorna to Porta Genova and walk south to the **Navigli** (▷ 96). Take a stroll along the towpaths on either side of the canal before dining at **El Brellín** or **Al Pont de Ferr** (▷ 105).

Evening Seek out one of the increasing number of popular nightspots concealed in the side streets of this district.

Top 25

▶ ▶ ▶

Arco della Pace ▷ **64**
Triumphal arch in memory
of the European peace
of 1815.

**Basilica di Sant'
Ambrogio** ▷ **82–83** A
prototype for Lombardian
Romantic-style churches.

Ca' Granda ▷ **44–45**
Fine tribute to 15th-century
Milan, now housing State
University departments.

**Villa Belgiojoso
Bonaparte** ▷ **30–31** A
wonderful neoclassical gallery
surrounded with gardens.

Teatro alla Scala ▷ **52**
One of the world's most
famous opera houses, which
remains the cultural focus
for the city's well-to-do.

**Santa Maria della
Passione** ▷ **97** Exquisite
art in Milan's second-largest
church after the Duomo.

Santa Maria delle Grazie
▷ **72–73** Da Vinci's
masterpiece is here in the
refectory of this significant
church.

San Maurizio ▷ **71**
The church exterior does
not do justice to the superb
frescoes displayed inside.

San Lorenzo Maggiore
▷ **86** Early Christian basilica concealing a superb interior and wonderful frescoes.

Quadrilatero d'Oro
▷ **28–29** Enticing shop-
window displays at the heart
of the fashion industry.

Pinacoteca di Brera
▷ **27** One of Italy's top
galleries, and the focus of
most visitors to the Brera.

Pinacoteca Ambrosiana
▷ **51** The oldest art
gallery in Milan, founded by
Cardinal Federico Borromeo.

These pages are a quick guide to the Top 25, which are described in more detail later. Here they are listed alphabetically, and the tinted background shows which area they are in.

THE NORTHEAST 21–40

PORTA ENAGLIA

Giardini Pubblici

BRERA   Pinacoteca di Brera
Orto Botanico

Villa Belgiojoso Bonaparte

QUADRILATERO D'ORO
PORTA MONFORTE

Museo Bagatti Valsecchi

Museo Poldi Pezzoli

Teatro lla Scala
Galleria Vittoria Emanuele II

Santa Maria della Passione

iazza Mercanti   Duomo

Palazzo Reale

Ca'Granda   Giardino Guastalla

STORICO CENTRO 41–60

◀ ◀ ◀

ESSENTIAL MILAN TOP 25

9

Shopping

Said to be the world's design capital, a visit to Milan's sensational fashion district is high on many visitors' itineraries, and designer clothes can cost less here than in New York or London.

The Golden Quad

Milan's most popular shopping area for *haute couture* is without doubt the network of pretty streets known as The Golden Quad, bordered by Via Montenapoleone, Via Manzoni, Via Sant'Andrea and Via Spiga. Here you will find designer clothes, accessories, shoes and leatherwear presented in chic, minimalist interiors that are works of art themselves. Even when the shops are closed, the streets are full of visitors admiring the window displays.

Other Options

You can also shop for superior goods at the glass-domed Galleria Vittorio Emanuele II (▷ 48); the bohemian Corso di Porta Ticinese, where there are smaller, trendy boutiques; or the up-and-coming Isola area, with some interesting boutiques. There are plenty of less elite stores selling more affordable items around Corso Vittorio Emanuele II, Via Torino, Corsa di Porta Romana and Corso Buenos Aires.

Interior Design Excellence

Milan is also at the forefront of interior design, ranging from the elegant to the wacky. Large

Shopping is the number one pleasure in Milan, be it for the latest designer creation, a succulent melon or tomatoes on the vine

FACTORY OUTLETS

If you are unable to pay the high prices of Milan's fashion district, don't despair. Factory outlets, stores that offer last season's products at a fraction of the price, are becoming very popular in Milan. Although, as the city has a reputation to uphold as one of the world's most important fashion hubs, many of the biggest designers are reluctant to put their name to outlet stores because they don't wish to be seen selling their creations at discount prices. You can also pick up sensational bargains during the end of season sales (January/February or July/August).

ultramodern showrooms stocked with original trendsetting items are apparent throughout the city. Smaller items that can easily be taken home include kitchen gadgets, decorated glass and sleek, stylish lighting.

Traditional Gifts

If you are looking for some traditionally Milanese products to take home, try some *panettone* (▷ panel below) or pick up a bottle of fine Italian wine from a reputable *enoteche*, where every purchase is beautifully wrapped and you can usually sample before you buy. For that special gift, head to one of the delightful stationery shops that stock hand-crafted paper-based products. The items are produced using luxury paper, hand-made from such materials as silk, coconut, lace and bamboo, in every hue and shade. They will need to be carefully packed for the journey home.

Antique Heaven

Antiques enthusiasts will enjoy browsing in the numerous antiques shops around the Brera district and along the canals, where regular antiques markets (▷ 90) are held. Shops specializing in old and new prints and lithographs, art galleries and auction houses are plentiful in Milan. For book lovers, the city has more than its fair share of spacious well-stocked bookshops, some selling books in many languages. There are also smaller, specialist bookshops that stock rare or out-of-print books.

PANETTONE

This famous Milanese cake, made with eggs, flour, sugar, candied fruits and spices, is now served at Christmas throughout Italy. It is said to have originated in the 15th century when the dessert at the Christmas Eve banquet for Ludovico Sforza was burned. It was rescued by Toni, a kitchen boy, who salvaged the remains of the burnt cake and added new ingredients. Since that day 'pan del Toni' became known as *panettone* and has remained popular ever since.

Shopping by Theme

Whether you're looking for a department store, a quirky boutique, or something in between, you'll find it all in Milan. On this page shops are listed by theme. For a more detailed write-up, see the individual listings in Milan by Area.

Milan by Night

After-hours entertainment in cosmopolitan Milan is vibrant; the city is known for Italy's hippest nightlife. If you prefer a slower pace, the city offers world-class opera, ballet and a theatre season that is the best and most varied in Italy. For the more energetic, there are glitzy nightclubs, trendy bars, disco-pubs, lively cafés and live music venues.

What's Hot

None of this is evident until after dark, when Milan's partygoers come out to play and the streets are thronged with beautiful people. Evenings usually begin slowly, with the *passeggiata*, where everyone struts up and down the central streets, mainly around Galleria Vittorio Emanuele II and the pedestrian zones along Via Dante. As the pace picks up, two popular areas to visit are the Navigli, or canal area, which is bisected by waterways and dotted with *osterie*, jazz bars and clubs, and the atmospheric Brera district, with intimate cafés, restaurants and clubs in its narrow cobbled streets.

A Little Culture

Opera fans will want to attend a performance at La Scala, Milan's famous opera house. The season runs from December to July, but performances sell out fast. There are many other places to enjoy classical music in the city, as well as live theatre, cultural events and a wide repertoire of plays. The city's many cinemas often show the new releases ahead of other Italian cities.

Opera and all that jazz. You can find it all in Milan, with great music venues and places just for a drink

---

DISCO-PUBS

Milan has a breed of pub popular with those who want to dance without being plunged into the noise and flashing lights of a full-blown disco; these are known as disco-pubs. Disco-pubs are ideal if you prefer to start the evening with a relaxing drink and quiet conversation, slowly building up to a party mood. Later into the evening the volume is turned up and the pub really starts to swing as every available space is taken up by disco divas performing the latest dance moves.

Eating Out

Eating is definitely one of life's pleasures in Milan. The diversity of Italy is as apparent in its food as it is in its culture and landscape. Whether you're after restaurants specializing in food from all over Italy or in international cooking, Milan can cater to all taste buds.

Meals and Mealtimes

Many working Milanese eat breakfast in a bar (a cappuccino and a sweet pastry). The day starts early, so if you are heading for breakfast in a bar, most open for business around 7–7.30. Hotels usually serve a buffet breakfast complete with fruit juice, cereal, cold meats and cheeses, which normally starts at 8, or earlier in business hotels. Lunch and dinner comprise *antipasto* (starter), *il primo* (pasta, risotto or soup), *secondo* (fish or meat) with *contorni* (vegetables) on the side, and *dolci* (dessert) or cheese. There's no pressure to wade through the whole menu; it's quite acceptable to order just one or two courses.

Where to Eat

Trattorie/osterie are usually family-run, serving simple authentic cooking and open during lunchtime and in the evening. But nowadays the name *osteria* is being adopted by smarter, trendy restaurants (▷ 92). *Ristoranti* are more upmarket and are not always open for lunch. *Pizzerie* (▷ 59) specialize in pizzas, but often serve simple pasta dishes as well. Some establishments still try to add a cover charge, which includes bread, and a service charge to the bill.

SNACKS

Bars serve hot and cold drinks, alcohol and snacks throughout the day. It's customary to eat or drink standing up; you will pay extra to sit down. Make your request and pay at the cash desk, then take the receipt and go to the bar where you will be served. *Távole calde* are stand-up snack bars that serve freshly prepared hot food. *Gelateria* (▷ 40) sell a range of ice cream, served in a cone or tub. The best ice cream is made on the premises.

Eat in style—Milan is a great place for dining alfresco, for coffee, lunch or a delectable ice cream

Restaurants by Cuisine

There are restaurants to suit all tastes and budgets in Milan. On this page they are listed by cuisine. For a more detailed description of each restaurant, see Milan by Area.

CAFÉS/BARS

Biffi (▷ 78)
Bindi (▷ 78)
Caffè Martini (▷ 59)
Caffè Real (▷ 59)
Caffè Sforzesco (▷ 59)
Cova (▷ 39)
Emporio Armani (▷ 39)
Marchesi (▷ 60)
Sant'Ambroeus (▷ 60)
Victoria Caffè (▷ 60)
Zucca in Galleria (▷ 60)

ELEGANT/TRENDY

Aimo e Nadia (▷ 105)
Bice (▷ 39)
Bvlgari (▷ 39)
Chandelier (▷ 105)
Il Sambuco (▷ 105)
Just Cavelli Café (▷ 78)
L'Amour (▷ 39)
Le 5 Terre (▷ 40)
Santini (▷ 40)
Savini (▷ 60)

FISH/VEGETARIAN

Asso di Fiori (▷ 105)
Da Gaspare (▷ 105)
Il Consolare (▷ 78)
Joia (▷ 39)
La Cozzeria (▷ 106)
La Terrazza (▷ 40)

ICE CREAM

Gelateria le Colonne (▷ 92)
Il Gabbiano (▷ 59)
La Bottega del Gelato (▷ 106)
Orsi (▷ 106)
Viel (▷ 78)

INTERNATIONAL

Ciriboga (▷ 92)
Copacabana (▷ 105)
Locando Greco (▷ 106)
Nobu (▷ 40)
Rangoli (▷ 40)
Shangri-la (▷ 40)
Spice (▷ 106)
Tandur (▷ 60)
Unco (▷ 106)
Yar (▷ 60)

MILANESE/ITALIAN

Al Mercante (▷ 59)
Arturoas la Latteria (▷ 39)
Cantina della Vetra (▷ 92)
Cracco Peck (▷ 59)
El Brellín (▷ 105)
Il Rosa al Caminetto (▷ 60)
La Tavernetta da Elio (▷ 39)
Mauro il Bolognese (▷ 106)
Orient Express (▷ 78)
Ristorante Sant'Eustorgio (▷ 92)
Rocking Horse (▷ 78)
Solferino (▷ 40)
Sudd (▷ 92)

PIZZERIA

All'Isola (▷ 78)
Be Bop (▷ 92)
Charleston (▷ 59)
Dai Damm (▷ 59)
Di Gennaro (▷ 59)
Tradizionale (▷ 106)
Transatlantico (▷ 40)

TRATTORIA/OSTERIA

Al Pont de Ferr (▷ 105)
C'Era Una Volta (▷ 78)
Il Giardinetto (▷ 92)
Le Vigne (▷ 106)
Osteria dei Binari (▷ 92)
Ponte Rosso (▷ 106)
Trattoria All'Antica (▷ 92)
Trattoria Milanese (▷ 60)

If You Like...

However you'd like to spend your time in Milan, these top suggestions should help you tailor your ideal visit. Each sight or listing has a fuller write-up in Milan by Area.

CUTTING-EDGE DESIGN

Cruise the Quadrilatero d'Oro (▷ 28–29) to see window displays presenting designers' creations straight off the catwalk.
Step inside shops like Dolce & Gabbana (▷ 36) on Via della Spiga and be amazed by the innovative interior designs.
Eat at Roberto Cavalli's steel and glass restaurant (▷ 78), decked out in his own pioneering designs.
Bring your home into the 21st century with a trendsetting item from De Driade (▷ 36).

Up-to-the-minute window displays in Milan (above)

ESCAPING THE HEAT AND NOISE

Lose yourself among the vast lawns and park-land of Parco Sempione (▷ 70).
If you really want to escape the city, head for Lake Como (▷ 101), only an hour away by train.
Take a diversion around the corner from Milan's exclusive shopping area to Giardini Pubblici (▷ 24).
Wander along the towpath of the canals (▷ 96) and find an *osteria* for lunch.

A GOOD NIGHT OUT

La Scala (▷ 58) is a must for a night to remember; book well in advance.
Have a meal and catch a late-night showing at the Odeon (▷ 58).
Start the evening early by joining 'happy hour' (▷ 91), or with a cocktail at Jamaica (▷ 77) then on to Hollywood (▷ 77) till the early hours.
Join the football-crazy Milanese to see AC or Inter play at the San Siro (▷ 103); discuss the game afterward over a drink at Bar Magenta (▷ 77).

A stroll in the park (above). Ticket for the opera (right)

Plenty of choices on the menus in Milan

A TASTE OF TRADITION

Fraternize with the locals at Trattoria Milanese (▷ 60); nearly a century of tradition is crammed into this homey restaurant.

Sample a taste of old Milan under beamed ceilings or on the shady terrace at El Brellín (▷ 105).

For excellent food that lives up to the Milanese tradition try Solferino (▷ 40).

Arturoas la Latteria (▷ 39) is one of the best examples of good regional cooking in Milan.

YOUR COFFEE IN STYLE

You won't be able to resist Biffi's (▷ 78) mouthwatering chocolate cake.

Cova (▷ 39) is a great place to rest your weary feet from the perils of excessive shopping.

Enyoy a touch of people-watching with your cappuccino at Zucca (▷ 60).

Take your pit-stop at the Emporio Armani Caffè (▷ 39) if you want to see and be seen—it's one of the most fashionable spots in town.

THE DOLCI VITA

Join an elite clientele for some luxurious pampering at Principe di Savoia (▷ 112).

Stylish eating is the order of the day in the city

Book one of the rooms with chromotherapy, aromatherapy and Japanese massage chaise longues at the Straf (▷ 112).

Endulge yourself in sumptuous surroundings haunted by royals and celebrities at the Grand Hotel de Milan (▷ 112).

Stay at the opulent Four Seasons hotel (▷ 112) in a 14th-century monastery set around a cloistered courtyard.

Elaborate oriental decoration on the table (left)

HOME-GROWN DESIGNERS

A stylish suit from the maestro. Fun and games at the workshop (below)

Visit at least one of Giorgio Armani's stores
(▷ 35), scattered throughout the Quad.
There's a Dolce & Gabbana
(▷ 36) around every street corner.
Treat yourself at Roberto Cavalli
(▷ panel 37), then flaunt your purchase at Just Cavalli Café (▷ 78).
Spoil your feet after all that walking;
Salvatore Ferragamo (▷ 37) has just
the thing.

FUN WITH THE KIDS

Learn about creatures from
under the water at the newly
renovated Acquario (▷ 74).
Try the hands-on exhibits at
the Science and Technology
Museum (▷ 84–85).
Allow the kids to let off steam in
Parco Sempione (▷ 70), and then have a picnic.
Sit on swivelling seats and gaze at the stars in
the Planetarium (▷ 24).

IF FUNDS ARE SHORT

Visit the city's free museums, which include
Museo di Milano (▷ 32).
Save up to 25 per cent at one of Milan's designer
factory outlets (▷ 10).
If you're likely to use public transport, buy a
travel card (▷ 118), its cheaper.
Consider staying at Hotel Due Giardini
(▷ 109) for good value for money.

*Take a tram to the Brera
and then go dancing*

SOMEWHERE TO DANCE

Rub shoulders with celebs at
Tocqueville (▷ 77).
The bank vaults come alive at La
Banque (▷ 58).
Drop in on one of Old Fashion Café's
(▷ 77) theme nights.
Try your hand at Latin-American
dancing at Tropicana Club Latino
(▷ 104).

Milan by Area

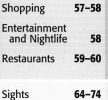

A

The northeast reflects the diverse nature of Milan. At its heart are the chic designer shops for which the city is so famous. Alongside are elegant *palazzi*, interesting museums and a tranquil park.

Giardini Pubblici

Take your pick—summer rides in the Giardini Pubblici make a welcome change

THE BASICS

➕ J3
✉ Corso Venezia, Via Manin, Via Palestro
🕐 6.30am–dusk
🍴 Café/bar
🚇 Turati, Palestro, Porta Venezia, Repubblica
🚌 94; tram 1, 2, 29, 30
♿ Good
🎟 Free

Planetarium

➕ K4
✉ Corso Venezia 57, 20121
☎ 02 8846 3340
🕐 Tue, Thu 9pm, Sat, Sun 3pm and 4.30pm
🚇 Porta Venezia,
🚌 Tram 9, 29, 30
♿ Good
🎟 Moderate

HIGHLIGHTS

● Museo del Cinema (▷ 32)
● Museo di Storia Naturale (▷ 33)
● Planetarium

The largest gardens in Milan were created on the lines of an English park. The attractions and summer entertainment, set among vast greenery and vibrant blooms, are a real breath of fresh air for adults and children alike.

Peace and tranquillity The public gardens extend for about 160,000sq m (192,000sq yards) and were designed by Guiseppe Piermarini in 1786. They were enlarged in 1857 by Guiseppe Balzaretto to include the Palazzo Dugnani and the Villa Belgiojoso Bonaparte (▷ 30–31). Further changes were made by Emilio Alemagna for the International Expo of 1871, incorporating waterfalls and fountains. Nowadays the gardens provide a welcome escape from the city heat and noise, and attract many joggers and family picnickers. In summer donkey rides, minitrain rides and a merry-go-round keep children amused for hours.

Not just a park Within the Palazzo Dugnani on the west side of the gardens is the small Museo del Cinema (▷ 32), with a collection of film- and camera-related items. On the east side is the Museo di Storia Naturale (▷ 33), popular for its reconstructed dinosaur collection.

View the stars Next to the natural history museum is the Planetario Ulrico Hoepli. The Planetarium was built in 1930 and is the biggest in Italy. It has a huge domed room where projections take place. Themes change monthly—call or check details at the tourist office.

Stunning blue and white patterned floor at the Museo Bagatti Valsecchi

Museo Bagatti Valsecchi

This charming museum, in a neo-Renaissance palace, houses fascinating antiques and curios and an extraordinary collection of genuine and reproduction furnishings of the brothers Fausto and Giuseppe Bagatti Valsecchi.

Ardent collectors Fausto and Giuseppe Bagatti Valsecchi, born respectively in 1843 and 1845, inherited their artistic flair from their father, a famous miniaturist. Using a large team of Lombard artisans, they skilfully renovated two *palazzi* (one in Via Gesù, the other backing onto it in Via Santo Spirito) between 1876 and 1895, to be used as their own home. Descendants of the brothers lived here until 1974 and created the Fondazione Bagatti Valsecchi, to open the collection to the public. It is now owned by the state.

Genuine or reproduction? You can visit the brothers' private apartments and the formal rooms they shared: the drawing room, hall of arms, dining room, study and Santo Spirito atrium. The Renaissance setting can be quite convincing—as can be the reproduction furniture that is integrated with the authentic pieces. The Camera Rossa has a charming display of 15th- to 17th-century children's furniture, while the dining room contains tapestries, sideboards and kitchenware. The library contains a number of important and valuable 15th-century parchments. In the Valtellinese bedroom there is a wonderful 16th-century bed with finely carved scenes of *The Road to Calvary* and Old Testament scenes together with paintings by Giampietrino.

THE BASICS

www.
museobagattivalsecchi.org
H5
Via Santo Spirito 10, 20121
02 7600 6132
Tue–Sun 1–5.45.
Usually closed New Year's Day, 6 Jan, Easter, 25 Apr, 1 May, 15 Aug, 1 Nov, 25 Dec, but changes each year
Montenapoleone
61, 94; tram 1, 2
None
Moderate
Every room has detailed sheets of information, translated into 6 languages. Good guidebook

HIGHLIGHTS

● Sala dell'Affresco, named after the fresco by Antonio Boselli of the *Madonna della Misericorda* (1496)
● Library, with painted leather celestial globe
● Valtellinese Bedroom
● The Red Bedroom—Painting of *Santa Giustina de' Borromei*, Giovanni Bellini (c1475)

Museo Poldi Pezzoli

TOP 25

The Gondola on the Lagoon *by Francesco Guardi (1712–93), in the Museo Poldi Pezzoli*

THE BASICS

www.museopoldipezzoli.it

⊞ H5

✉ Via Manzoni 12, 20121

☎ 02 794 889

🕐 Tue–Sun 10–6; closed
1 Jan, Easter, 25 Apr, 1 May,
1 & 15 Aug, 1 Nov, 8, 25 &
26 Dec

Ⓜ Montenapoleone

🚌 61, 94; tram 1, 2,

♿ Poor but ground floor
possible

💶 Expensive

ℹ Audiotours, shop

The palace and its exquisite collection of paintings and decorative arts belonged to Gian Giacomo Poldi Pezzoli, a 19th-century Milanese aristocrat. Each room was planned to evoke a style of the past.

Stunning collection With the considerable fortune inherited from both sides of the family, Poldi Pezzoli (1822–79) amassed a large collection of antiques and art, the nucleus of which was his remarkable armoury. With the advice of leading experts, Poldi Pezzoli built up a collection of armour, furniture, textiles, ceramics, bronzes and objets d'art. Pride of place, however, goes to his fabulous collection of paintings. On his death, he left the palace and its contents 'to the use and benefit of the public'. The building was badly bombed in 1943, but was rebuilt, retaining the original decoration where possible. Through gifts and bequests, the museum considerably enlarged its collection in the 1970s and 1980s.

Art and arms The two floors of exhibits are connected by a charming staircase with landscape paintings and a black marble fountain. The ground-floor rooms are devoted to the Armoury, in its stunning neo-Gothic setting, the Fresco Room, the textile collections and library. The main collections are upstairs: paintings from the 14th- to 16th-century Lombard School, northern Italian works of art from the 14th–18th centuries and the Salone Dorato, or Golden Room, which is full of Renaissance masterpieces. Further rooms display jewellery, sundials, clocks and watches.

HIGHLIGHTS

In the Salone Dorato:
● *Portrait of a Young Woman*, Piero del Pollaiuolo—this lovely portrait has become a symbol of the palace.
● *Pietà and Madonna and Child*, Sandro Botticelli
● *St. Nicholas of Tolentino*, Piero della Francesca
● *Madonna and Child*, Andrea Mantegna
● *Pietà*, Giovanni Bellini

TOP 25

THE NORTHEAST

Canova's statue of Napoleon (left). The Kiss by Francesco Hayez (right)

Pinacoteca di Brera

The Brera gallery offers the chance to see one of the finest collections of northern Italian paintings. From small beginnings, it was enlarged by Napoleon to include works by the region's major artists.

Impressive collection The gallery is in the Palazzo Brera, a baroque palace built on the site of a 14th-century Jesuit convent. Empress Maria Theresa of Austria evicted the Jesuits, redesigned the palace in neoclassical style and founded the Accademia di Belle Arti in 1773. The Pinacoteca opened in 1809, showing mostly works that had been confiscated by Napoleon from churches and convents in French-occupied territories: Lombardy, Veneto, Emilia-Romagna and the Marche. Through donations and exchanges, the collection has been growing ever since. In 1882, the Accademia di Belle Arti and the Pinacoteca became independent, and the gallery became a state-owned art museum.

An art lover's heaven The works of art are arranged in 38 large rooms, making for pleasant viewing. Although the collection spans six centuries and includes some non-Italian artists (El Greco, Anthony Van Dyck, Rubens, Rembrandt), the emphasis is on northern Italian 15th- to 16th-century art. The collection is full of gems by the leading Renaissance masters, with the Venetian collection the largest and most important outside Venice. Here, too, you have a chance to study the Lombard masters of the Renaissance. The two most famous paintings in the collection are by Piero della Francesca and Raphael (▷ Highlights).

THE BASICS

www.brera.beniculturali.it
✚ G4
✉ Via Brera 28, 20121
☎ 02 722 631
🕐 Tue–Sun 8.30–7.15 (last admission 45 mins before closing). Closed 1 Jan, 1 May, 25 Dec
🚇 Lanza, Montenapoleone
🚌 61; tram 1, 27
♿ Good, elevator
💲 Moderate
ℹ Audiotours, good book and souvenir shop

HIGHLIGHTS

● Jesi Collection–paintings and sculpture from the first half of the 19th century
● *Marriage of the Virgin* (1504), Raphael
● *Montefeltro Altarpiece* (1472–74), Piero della Francesca
● *Dead Christ*, Mantegna
● Portraits by Lotto, Tintoretto, Titian
● *Virgin of the Rose Garden*, Bernardino Luini
● *The Kiss*, Francesco Hayez

Quadrilatero d'Oro

HIGHLIGHTS

● Cova at Via
Montenapoleone 8 (▷ 39),
a historic café with tantalizing window displays of patisserie, sweets and chocolates.
Sip coffee at the bar or sit in
one of the smart salons with
well-dressed Milanese.
● One of the best spots in
Europe to window shop
● Aristocratic residences

TIP

● Make an early start to
avoid the crowds, but most
shops won't open before
9.30am.

**Milan is Italy's high spot for fashion and
the area known as the Quadrilatero d'Oro
(The Golden Quad), northeast of the
Duomo, is the most exclusive shopping
quarter of the city. All the top designer
names are here.**

Glitz and glamour The Quadrilatero d'Oro is
defined by Via Montenapoleone, Via Manzoni, Via
della Spiga and Via Sant'Andrea. Via Manzoni is
wide and traffic laden, the other streets in the
shopping quarter are relatively quiet and make for
pleasant shopping and give the opportunity just to
window shop. Via Montenapoleone, familiarly
known as Montenapo, is the most famous of
these exclusive streets, lined with elegant clothing
stores including Ferragamo, Armani, Valentino,
Prada and Versace, and high-class jewellers.

A feast for the designer fashion lover as the stores flaunt the latest styles (left). Sexy black lace underwear displayed at La Perla (middle). It's a serious business shopping in Milan and even the most seasoned shopper needs plenty of stamina and a good list (right)

Palaces, courtyards and museums The name Quadrilatero d'Oro comes from the early 19th century and the quarter still preserves some of its historic *palazzi* as well as some fascinating courtyards. Via Bigli has the oldest buildings, with some of the palaces dating back to the 17th century. The shopping district is also home to the Museo Bagatti Valsecchi (▷ 25) and two civic museums, both at Via Sant'Andrea 6: the Museo di Milano (▷ 32) and the Museo di Storia Contemporanea (Contemporary History).

Milan style Don't expect a bargain unless you come during the January sales; the prices here tend to be higher than the rest of the city. The window fronts are stylish, artfully displaying the latest trends in fashion, as well as showcasing jewellery, fine leather, luxury furs and accessories.

THE BASICS

✚ H4

✉ 20121

🕐 Varied. Most shops close on Sun and Mon, though some are open on Mon afternoon. Most open at 9am or 9.30am

🍴 Numerous, with some very chic ones

🚇 San Babila, Montenapoleone

🚌 61, 94; tram 1, 2,

♿ Good

Villa Belgiojoso Bonaparte

 TOP 25

TIP

● Choose a sunny, or at least dry day, to visit the Villa and its gardens. You will be close to the Giardini Pubblici for a walk or picnic afterward.

This vast neoclassical villa has been occupied by Napoleon and Josephine, Count Joseph Radetzky (the Austrian commander-in-chief) and the Italian royal family. Part is now home to the Museo dell'Ottocento (19th-century museum).

Famous residents The Villa was built in 1790 by Leopold Pollack for Count Ludovico Barbiano di Belgiojoso. After the count's death in the early 19th century, the Italian Government donated it as a residence for Napoleon and Josephine, and it passed into the hands of the city of Milan in 1921.

Milanese collectors Occupying 35 rooms, the Museo dell'Ottocento illustrates the main artistic movements of the 19th and early 20th century, with emphasis on Italian and French art. The

Il Quarto Stato (The Fourth Estate) by Guiseppe Pellizza da Polpedo, depicting the workers' march. The painting is displayed in the Museo dell'Ottocento, which is located in the Villa Belgiojoso Bonaparte, on the edge of Giardini Pubblici

rooms cover from the neoclassical period to Romanticism, from the Scapigliatura (a Milan-based movement) through Divisionism to Realism. The three most important collections are the Grassi, Vismara and Marino. The Marino Marini Collection opened in 1973 and contains bronzes, portrait busts and drawings by the Italian sculptor Marini (1901–80). Some of the busts depict the artist's friends and acquaintants (among them Ivor Stravinsky, Henry Miller, Henry Moore and Marc Chagall) and are remarkable for their psychological insight.

Beyond the walls The small building beside the villa is the Padiglione d'Arte Contemporanea (PAC), which hosts temporary modern art exhibitions. There are good views of the English-style gardens from the upper floors of the villa.

THE BASICS

www.
villabegiojosobonaparte.it
⊞ J4
✉ Via Palestro 16, 20121
☎ 02 7600 2819/7780 9761
🕐 Tue–Sun 9–1, 2–5.30 (last admission 5)
🚇 Palestro
🚌 61, 94; tram 1, 2
♿ Good
🎟 Free

More to See

ARCHI DI PORTA NUOVA

The large, double-arched gateway separates Via Manzoni and Piazza Cavour. This and Porta Ticinese are the only surviving gates of the medieval walls that protected the city.

🚩 H4 ✉ North end of Via Manzoni, 20121
🚇 Montenapoleone 🚌 61, 94; tram 1, 2

BASTIONI DI PORTA VENEZIA

On the site of one of the Porte Regie (Royal Gates) in the Spanish city walls, constructed in the 16th century, the present-day arch dates from 1828.

🚩 K3 ✉ Piazza Oberdan, 20129 🚇 Porta Venezia 🚌 Tram 9, 29, 30

MUSEO DEL CINEMA

www.cinetecamilano.it

This small museum is packed with weird and wonderful magic lanterns, early-19th-century pre-camera viewers, antique snapshot cameras, early examples of cine cameras and vintage posters of Hollywood and Italian movie stars. A tiny cinema shows old films and cartoons for children at weekends.

🚩 J4 ✉ Palazzo Dugnani, Via Manin 2/b, 20121 ☎ 02 655 4977 🕐 Fri–Sun 3–6 (films at 4–5; reservations essential)
🚇 Turati 🚌 61, 94; tram 1, 2 ♿ Good (narrow access path) 💶 Moderate

MUSEO DI MILANO

www.museidelcentro.mi.it

Together with the Museo di Storia Contemporanea, an exhibition space for modern history and lectures, the Museo di Milano is located in the Palazzo Morando Attendolo Bolognini. The rooms of the 18th century palace display the original furniture and décor and recall a typical noble family's residence. On show are paintings, prints and objects recalling the past of the city from the 18th century until the end of the 19th century.

🚩 J5 ✉ Via Sant'Andrea 6, 20121 ☎ 02 7600 6245 🕐 Tue–Sun 2–5.30
🚇 Montenapoleone 🚌 61, 94; tram 1, 2
♿ Good 💶 Free

MUSEO DEL RISORGIMENTO

www.museidelcentro.mi.it

This museum is in the neoclassical Palazzo Moriggia and traces Italy's

Roman tombstones from the first century AD in the Archi di Porta Nuova

Deer statues outside the Natural History Museum

history from Napoleon's campaigns in Italy (1796 and 1800) to Unification in 1866. Exhibits include prints and paintings, original documents, busts, mementos and proclamations. You can see the first Italian flag (Primo Tricolore), which was used at the Battle of Arcole Bridge in 1796.

🚺 H4 ✉ Via Borgonuovo 23, 20121 ☎ 02 8846 4176 ⏱ Tue–Sun 9–1, 2–5.30 🚇 Montenapoleone 🚌 61; tram 1, 2 ♿ Good 💰 Moderate, free on Fri after 2

MUSEO DI STORIA NATURALE

Occupying 23 rooms of a huge mock-Romanesque late-19th-century building on the edge of the Giardini Pubblici, this museum has sections on geology, mineralogy, palaeontology, entomology, zoology and habitats. Children will be drawn to the dinosaurs and the life-size reproductions of crocodiles, snakes and sea creatures. Explanations in Italian only.

🚺 K4 ✉ Corso Venezia 55, 20121 ☎ 02 8846 3337 ⏱ Tue–Sun 9–6 🚇 Palestro 🚌 Tram 9, 30 ♿ Good 💰 Moderate, free on Fri after 2

PALAZZO SERBELLONI

This monumental neoclassical palace has played host to famous historical figures such as Napoleon and Josephine and King Vittorio Emanuele II, among others. It was built in 1793, and was partially restored after the bombings in World War II. During office hours, you can walk through the huge arched entrance to the frescoed loggia and arcaded courtyard.

🚺 J5 ✉ Corso Venezia 16, 20121 ⏱ View from outside only 🚇 San Babila 🚌 61

SAN MARCO

Built in 1254, the present church was founded on the site of the 12th-century church of San Marco. It was designed in Romanesque style, but underwent major Gothic and baroque transformations—plus 19th-century restoration. The main portal, with bas-reliefs, and the tower, with decorative friezes (only seen from Via Pontaccio), survive from the 13th-century church.

🚺 G4 ✉ Piazza San Marco 2, 20121 ☎ 02 2900 2598 ⏱ Daily 7.30–1, 4–7.15 🚌 61, 43 ♿ Few 💰 Free

Detail of the first vault in the presbytery of San Marco

From Retail to Calm

Window-shop till you drop in Milan's bustling fashion quarter and then take a well-earned rest in the public gardens.

DISTANCE: 3.2km (2 miles) **ALLOW:** Half a day to include shopping and sights

START

VIA MONTENAPOLEONE
🔲 H5 🚇 Montenapoleone

END

GARDINI PUBBLICI
🔲 J3 🚇 Porta Venezia/Palestro

1 Begin on Via Montenapoleone, where it joins Via Manzoni. This is one of the best spots to window-shop in Europe, overflowing with top designer names and excellent coffee stops.

2 Explore the smaller streets to the left of Via Montenapoleone. At the end turn left and cross Piazza San Babila; then go left again into Corso Venezia.

3 Take the next left into Via Spiga for more exclusive shops. Halfway down cross over Via Sant'Andrea, home to the Museo di Milano (▷ 32).

4 Continue past Via Gesù on the left, on to Via Santo Spirito, also on the left, where you can visit the Museo Bagatti Valsecchi (▷ 25), with its superb interior furnishings.

8 Another attraction here is the Planetarium (▷ 24) in the far eastern corner. You can exit near here for the Porta Venezia metro.

7 The villa houses the Museo dell'Ottocento and is set in an English garden. Cross over the road and enter the Giardini Pubblici. Around the perimeter of the park are the museums of natural history (▷ 33) and cinema (▷ 32).

6 Turn right through the arch into Piazza Cavour. Cross the piazza and bear right into Via Palestro opposite the Giardini Pubblici (▷ 24). Halfway along here is the Villa Belgiojoso Bonaparte (▷ 30–31).

5 The end of the street brings you to the Archi di Porta Nuova (▷ 32).

WALK

THE NORTHEAST

Shopping

ACQUA DI PARMA
www.acquadiparma
Items to pamper the feet, body, face and scalp, and leather pouches in which to put your new purchases.
🔲 J5 ✉ 3 Via Gesù, 20121
☎ 02 7602 3307
🚇 Montenapoleone

ALAN JOURNO
www.alanjourno.com
Crazy bags, hats and lots more in eccentric styles displayed around a stainless steel and glass staircase that spirals over three levels.
🔲 J4 ✉ Via della Spiga 36, 20121 ☎ 02 7600 1309
🚇 Montenapoleone

ALEXANDER MCQUEEN
www.alexandermcqueen.com
Opened in 2003, this store reveals a series of interconnecting rooms to show off the designer's unique styles.
🔲 H5 ✉ Via Pietro Verri 8, 20121 ☎ 02 7600 3374
🚇 Montenapoleone

ANTICHITÀ CAIATI
www.caiati.it
This exclusive gallery specializes in Venetian landscapes and 17th- and 18th-century Italian paintings.
🔲 J5 ✉ Via Gesù 17, 20121
☎ 02 794 866
🚇 Montenapoleone

ARMANDOLA
An elegant deli that reflects its exclusive location in its prices. But the tempting aroma of cheese and the display of freshly made pastas and jars of truffles make it worth every penny.
🔲 J4 ✉ Via della Spiga 50, 20121 ☎ 02 7602 1657
🚇 Montenapoleone

ARMANI CASA
www.armanicasa.com
Yet another one for the Armani empire. No longer just fashion, Armani is synonomous with a whole lifestyle. Sophisticated, stylish furniture and lovely accessories for the home.
🔲 H4 ✉ Via Manzoni 37, 20121 ☎ 02 7231 8630
🚇 Montenapoleone

ARTEMIDE
www.artemide.com
Renowned for forthright modern designs for the

EMPIRE OF ARMANI

Milan-born designer Giorgio Armani began his career as a window dresser at the city's La Rinascente department store, and in 1961 progressed to the menswear shop Nino Cerruti. In 1975, Armani branched out alone, and within 10 years had become a household name when he revolutionized the industry with his more wearable and less-expensive collection. The Armani Empire took another giant leap forward in 2000, when it opened its flagship store, Emporio Armani, in Milan (✉ Via Manzoni 31, 2021 ☎ 02 7231 8605; www.emporioarmani.it).

---

home, created by top designers, the products are displayed to best effect in a gallery-like showroom.
🔲 J5 ✉ Corso Monforte 19, 20122 ☎ 02 7600 6930
🚇 San Babila

BVLGARI
www.bulgari.com
The Milan branch of the world-famous fashion jeweller and watchmaker.
🔲 J5 ✉ Via della Spiga 6, 20121 ☎ 02 7601 3448
🚇 San Babila

CARLO ORSI
The fine paintings, bronze sculpture, furniture and precious stones on sale here are a collector's dream.
🔲 J5 ✉ Via Bagutta 14, 20121 ☎ 02 7600 2214
🚇 San Babila

CARTIER
www.cartier.com
Police-guarded Cartier has gold, silver and porcelain that is the stuff of dreams, as are the prices.
🔲 H5 ✉ Corner Via Montenapoleone and Via Gesù 2, 20121 ☎ 02 3030 0421
🚇 San Babila

DAMIANI
www.damiani.it
Damiani have been creating bold designs using high-quality gems since 1924. Also classy watches, strings of pearls and fine wedding rings.
🔲 J5 ✉ Via Montenapoleone 10, 20121 ☎ 02 7602 8088 🚇 San Babila

DE DRIADE
www.driade.it
Founded in 1968, De Driade is always seeking new trends in home and office furniture, with some items going on to become collectors' items.
⊞ H4 ✉ Via Manzoni 30, 20121 ☎ 02 7602 3098
Ⓜ Montenapoleone

DE PADOVA
www.depadova.it
Elegance and simplicity of design are key at this shop for the discerning homeowner. You can be sure only the finest materials are used.
⊞ J5 ✉ Corso Venezia 14, 20121 ☎ 02 777 201 Ⓜ San Babila, Palestro

DOLCE & GABBANA
www.dolcegabbana.it
At the cutting edge of fashion and straight off the catwalk, this amazing store is worth a look for the décor alone.
⊞ J4 ✉ Via della Spiga 26 20121 ☎ 02 7600 1155
Ⓜ Montenapoleone

DROGHERIA PARINI
Upstairs for mouthwatering confectionery and downstairs to the arched cellar for wines and spirits, cookies, organic jams and jellies, compotes and chutneys, and excellent blends of coffee and tea—all beautifully gift-wrapped. Very friendly and helpful staff.
⊞ H4 ✉ Via Borgospesso 1, 20121 ☎ 02 7600 2303
Ⓜ Montenapoleone

FELTRINELLI INTERNATIONAL
This branch of the well-known bookstore is where the world's fashion hierarchy come to buy their English and American *Vogues*, *Elles* and *Cosmopolitans*. Good selection of travel books, too.
⊞ H4 ✉ Piazza Cavour 2, 20122 ☎ 02 659 5644
Ⓜ Turati

FENDI
www.fendi.com
From recent beginnings (in high-fashion furs), the Fendi sisters have built a powerful fashion, perfume and accessories empire. The clothes here are classic, sleek and stylish.
⊞ J5 ✉ Via Sant'Andrea 16, 20121 ☎ 02 7602 1617
Ⓜ San Babila

FLOS
www.flos.com
High-quality ultramodern lighting for the home and office, with contemporary creations by names such as Philippe Starck and Jasper Morrison.
⊞ J5 ✉ Corso Monforte 9, 20122 ☎ 02 7600 1641
Ⓜ San Babila

FRATELLI ROSSETTI
www.rossetti.it
This family company, founded 30 years ago by the brothers Renzo and Renato, pushes Salvatore Ferragamo (▷ 37) hard for the title of Italy's best shoe store. You'll find classic and current styles at slightly lower prices than its rival.
⊞ J5 ✉ Via Montenapoleone 1, 20121 ☎ 02 7602 1650
Ⓜ San Babila

JIL SANDER
www.jilsander.it
Avant-garde cuts and attention to detail are the trademarks of this famous German designer. Styles for both men and women.
⊞ H5 ✉ Via Pietro Verri 6, 20121 ☎ 02 777 2991
Ⓜ San Babila

KARTELL
Minimal moulded furnishings: bowls, cups, seats and lamp stands made almost entirely from bright and stunningly curved plastic.
⊞ H4 ✉ Via Carlo Porta 1, 20122 ☎ 02 659 7916
Ⓜ Turati

KRIZIA

Lower in the fashion firmament than Armani or Versace, but Krizia has a high profile in Italy, especially for knitwear.

H5 ✉ Via della Spiga 23, 20121 ☎ 02 7600 8429
Ⓜ San Babila

LA PERLA

www.laperla.it
Sultry and sophisticated underwear and swimwear, made in the finest fabrics.

H5 ✉ Via Montenapoleone 1, 20121 ☎ 02 7600 0460
Ⓜ San Babila

LAURA BIAGIOTTI

www.laurabiagiotti.it
Easy-to-wear fashion, gentle on the eye and less aggressively 'high fashion' than some other designers.

H4 ✉ Via Borgospesso 19, 20121 ☎ 02 799 659
Ⓜ Montenapoleone

LE SILLA

www.lesilla.com
A must for lovers of expensive shoes. Women's footwear, from the smart to the seductive and scandalous.

H5 ✉ Corso Venezia 8, 20121 ☎ 02 7600 5286
Ⓜ San Babila

MIRABELLO

The trade name Mirabello is a symbol of high quality and youthful design. The fun, fresh ideas encompass household linens, curtains, fabrics and more.

H3 ✉ Via Montebello (corner of Via San Marco), 20121 ☎ 02 654 887
Ⓜ Turati, Moscova

MIU MIU

Urban chic from the House of Prada. Check out the high-tech interior.

H5 ✉ Corso Venezia 3, 20121 ☎ 02 7601 4448
Ⓜ San Babila

N'OMBRA DE VIN

www.nombradevin.it
This shop has a fine collection of wines from Italy, France and the New World. You can taste before you make your decision to buy.

G4 ✉ Via San Marco 2, 20121 ☎ 02 659 9650
Ⓜ Turati, Moscova

DESIGNER HEAVEN

The concentration of designer stores in the Quadrilatero d'Oro is unbelievable. All the top names are here flaunting their latest catwalk designs. Check out Via Manzoni for Armani; Via Sant'Andrea for Chanel and Prada; Via Montenapoleone for Gucci, Louis Vitton, Versace and Yves Saint Laurent, and don't forget one of Italy's preferred sons, Robert Cavalli, with his signature animal skin designs on Via della Spiga. The prices may be high but it's free to window-shop. But be sure to go inside to see the crazy interiors of some stores or try on a least one special little number.

RANIERI

One of Milan's great patisserie institutions. The pineapple *panettone* is particularly good.

H3 ✉ Via della Moscova 7, 20121 ☎ 02 659 5308
Ⓜ Turati, Moscova

SALVATORE FERRAGAMO

www.salvatoreferragamo.it
Italy's most famous shoe designer, whose stores grace exclusive shopping streets all over the world.

H5 ✉ Via Montenapoleone 3, 20121 ☎ 02 7600 0054
Ⓜ San Babila

SERMONETA

www.sermonetagloves.com
Handmade leather gloves in every size, shade and style you can imagine.

H5 ✉ Via della Spiga 46, 20121 ☎ 02 7631 8303
San Babila

TIFFANY & CO

Legendary jewellers selling highly desirable crystals, gold and silverware, clocks and jewellery, but at prices that suit only the extremely rich.

H5 ✉ Via della Spiga 19a, 20121 ☎ 02 7602 2321
Ⓜ San Babila

VETRERIE DI EMPOLI

Gorgeous hand-decorated glasses, chandeliers, vases and fruit dishes: this shop is a must for glass collectors.

J4 ✉ Via Montenapoleone 14, 20121 ☎ 02 7600 8791
Ⓜ Montenapoleone

Entertainment and Nightlife

ANTEO

www.spaziocinema.com
One of Milan's leading original-language cinemas, with a slant on art house rather than mainstream pictures. Films from countries such as Sweden, Japan or France are often shown with English subtitles.
➕ G4 ✉ Via Milazzo 9, 20121 ☎ 02 659 7732
Ⓜ Moscova

DIANA MAJESTIC BAR

Partake of sophisticated cocktails and aperitifs in the bar at the Sheraton Diana Majestic hotel (▷ 112). Sit out in the elegant gardens during summer, while the lavish lounge and opulent bar are a great pit-stop in the cooler months.
➕ K4 ✉ Viale Piave 42, 20129 ☎ 02 20581
Ⓜ Porta Venezia

LELEPHANTE

www.lelephant.com
One of the city's leading hangouts for dressed-up revellers and trendy students. Decked out with innovative plastic furniture. Aimed at both the straight and gay crowd.
➕ L4 ✉ Via Melzo 22, 20129 ☎ 02 2951 8768
Ⓜ Porta Venezia

PISCINA COZZI

Located on the tree-lined Via Tunisia just north of the Giardini Pubblici, this swimming pool complex has two pools, one of which is Olympic size with 5m (16.4ft) and 10m (32.8ft) diving boards. It can get crowded in high season but it is the closest place in central Milan to cool off. Open every day but check in advance for session times.
➕ K3 ✉ Via Tunisia 35, 20124 ☎ 02 659 9703
Ⓜ Porta Venezia, Repubblica

TEATRO MANZONI

www.teatromanzoni.it
This theatre is particularly popular with the Milanese and produces a variety of performances, including serious drama such as plays by Chekhov and Brecht, Italian plays, one-man shows, stand-up comedy, classical music concerts and musicals; Sunday mornings for jazz.
➕ H4 ✉ Via Alessandro Manzoni 42, 20121 ☎ 02 763 6901 Ⓜ Montenapoleone

TICKET INFORMATION

Tickets for theatre and concerts can be booked through agencies and also from specialist booking offices such as the Ricordi Box Office in Galleria Vittorio Emanuele II (☎ 02 869 0683), in the Virgin Megastore in Piazza Duomo (☎ 02 7200 3370) and in the Stazione Centrale (☎ 02 669 6757). Tickets for La Scala need to be purchased well in advance—it may be possible on very rare occasions to get a ticket two hours before a performance.

TEATRO SAN BABILA

www.teatrosanbabila.it
Tradition is the key here, and the Milanese flock to see famous actors and directors stage their best-loved works of drama in this 500-seat performance venue. Be sure to reserve well in advance.
➕ J5 ✉ Corso Venezia 2/a, 20121 ☎ 02 7600 2985
Ⓜ San Babila

THAT'S AMORE

www.thatsamore.it
One of Milan's most respected bars, attracting fashionable drinkers of all ages. Sip your cocktails at the sleek, curvy silver bar. Early aperitifs may descend into dance floor revelry before the night is over.
➕ J3 ✉ Viale Monte Santo 8, 20124 ☎ 02 2906 0626
Ⓜ Repubblica

THE FRIENDS

www.thefriendsmilano.it
This is where to go if you are feeling nostalgic for an English pub; the building was even sent in parts from England. It is a popular venue for expats but for tourists, too. Lots of Victorian décor and all the beers and lagers you should want. There is live music on some Sundays—it is best to check in advance. Prices are already low but happy hour and self-service buffet runs from 6 until 9.
➕ J3 ✉ Viale Monte Santo 12, 20124 ☎ 02 2900 5315
Ⓜ Repubblica

Restaurants

ARTUROAS LA LATTERIA (€–€€)

Busy family-run restaurant serving food from the Lombardy region. Haunt of journalists and the occasional celebrity in search of good honest food.

➕ G3 ✉ Via San Marco 24, 20121 ☎ 02 659 7653 🕐 Mon–Fri lunch, dinner 🚇 Moscova

BICE (€€)

www.bicemilano.it
Founded in 1926, Bice is in one of the smartest streets in the fashion district and is popular with the Milanese élite. Extensive à la carte menu; lighter set menu for lunch.

➕ H4 ✉ Via Borgospesso 12, 20121 ☎ 02 7600 2572 🕐 Mon–Sat lunch, dinner 🚇 Montenapoleone

BVLGARI (€€€)

www.bulgarihotels.it
Mix with the seriously rich crowd at this smart restaurant in the Bvlgari hotel on the edge of the Orto Botanico. Gorgeous terrace and gardens.

➕ H4 ✉ Via Fratelli Gabba 7b, 20121 ☎ 02 805 8051 🕐 Daily lunch, dinner 🚇 Montenapoleone

COVA (€€)

In business since 1817, this landmark café is an ideal stop for a break from shopping. It is expensive but the coffee and cakes are irresistible.

➕ H5 ✉ Via Montenapoleone 8, 20121 ☎ 02 7600 0578 🕐 Mon–Sat all day 🚇 San Babila, Montenapoleone

EMPORIO ARMANI CAFFÈ (€€)

Why not take a break for a designer coffee, pastries, light lunches, juices or a cocktail after browsing this sleek store, the flagship of the famous designer.

➕ H4 ✉ Piazza Croce Rossa 2, 20121 ☎ 02 7231 8680 🕐 Mon–Sat all day 🚇 Montenapoleone

---

ANYONE FOR COFFEE?

The Milanese have coffees to suit different types of food or to be drunk at different times of day. Cappuccino, or the longer and milkier *caffè latte*, are often the choice at breakfast, followed by *espresso* for a short kick-start of caffeine later in the day. Not many visitors will risk the *ristretto*, as this is the strongest of them all. Cappuccino is never drunk by Italians after lunch or dinner. Other varieties are *caffè americano* (full cup and watery), *caffè freddo* (iced coffee) and *caffè macchiato* (*espresso* 'stained' with a dash of milk).

JOIA (€€€)

www.joia.it
Closeness to nature is the philosophy behind this first-class vegetarian restaurant, where the freshest of ingredients are lovingly prepared to tempt the palate.

➕ K3 ✉ Via P. Castaldi 18, 20124 ☎ 02 2952 2124 🕐 Mon–Fri lunch, dinner. Closed 3 weeks Aug 🚇 Repubblica, Porta Venezia

L'AMOUR (€€)

www.lamour.it
The perfect place for an after-show dinner in classic surroundings with an up-to-date twist. Warm ambience and subtle lighting to accompany your seafood, fish or meat main course. Yummy desserts to finish off with.

➕ G3 ✉ Via Solferino 25, 20121 ☎ 02 2952 2124 🕐 Tue–Sun lunch, dinner. Closed Aug 🚇 Moscova

LA TAVERNETTA DA ELIO (€€)

www.tavernetta.it
In the same family since 1957, this historic restaurant is preferred by celebrities and literary types. The cuisine is Tuscan in all its most traditional forms—thick soups, pastas and hearty meat dishes. Good desserts and Tuscan wines.

➕ H4 ✉ Via Fatebenefratelli 30, 20121 ☎ 02 7653 441 🕐 Mon–Fri lunch, dinner, Sat dinner only 🚇 Montenapoleone, Turati

THE NORTHEAST

RESTAURANTS

LA TERRAZZA (€€)

www.laterrazzadiviapalestro.it

Eat sushi on the top floor of this office block while taking in the great view over the Giardini Pubblici, especially on the terrace in summer.

J4 ✉ Via Palestro 2, 20121 ☎ 02 7600 2186 ⏰ Mon–Sat lunch, dinner 🚇 Lotto

LE 5 TERRE (€€–€€€)

www.ristorante5terre.it

In business for over 20 years, this restaurant is the master of Ligurian cuisine, particularly renowned for its fish dishes. Meat is more limited but although carnivores are catered for this is the place for real fish lovers. Leave room for the delicious desserts. The surroundings are elegant and the excellent wine list comprehensive.

H3 ✉ Via Andrea Appiani 9, 20121 ☎ 02 657 5177 ⏰ Daily lunch, dinner. Closed Sun in Aug and 10–25 Dec 🚇 Repubblica, Turati

NOBU (€€€)

www.giorgioarmani.it

Chef Nobuyuki Matsuhisa has been creating culinary treats for over 10 years in the Armani store. Here Japanese cuisine meets South American and Californian influences. Very smart and very expensive.

H4 ✉ Via Pisoni 1, 20121 ☎ 02 6231 2645 ⏰ Mon–Sat lunch, dinner; Sun dinner only 🚇 Montenapoleone

RANGOLI (€)

www.rangoli.it.

Authentic North Indian cuisine in the Brera district. The dishes cooked in the *tandoor* (clay oven) are particularly popular. There is a good vegetarian menu.

G3 ✉ Via Solferino 36, 20121 ☎ 02 2900 5333 ⏰ Sun–Fri lunch, dinner, Sat dinner only 🚇 Moscova

SANTINI (€€€)

www.ristorantesantini.it

This is the epitome of sophistication with cool, clean lines and modern lighting. The striking blue-and-white dining room is very distinctive. A full menu features fusion and Piedmont cuisine, or try light lunch options such as spaghetti or vegetable wraps. Alternatively you can opt for the special 'Taste of Santini' menu

ITALIAN ICE CREAM

The Italians justifiably pride themselves on their superior ice cream, and Milan regards itself as one of the best ice cream making areas in the country. There are *gelaterie* dating back to the mid-19th century that are still in business, some have as many as 100 different varieties on offer. Many make their ice cream with all natural ingredients and you often find a wonderful array of fresh fruits to accompany your choice.

featuring the chef's specials. There's a nice covered garden area for alfresco eating.

G3 ✉ Via San Marco 3, 20121 ☎ 02 655 5587 ⏰ Mon–Fri lunch, dinner, Sat lunch only 🚇 Lanza

SHANGRI-LA (€€)

Spicy Thai and traditional Chinese cooking at this restaurant north of the Giardini Pubblici. For something a little different try the fried rice served in half a pineapple.

K3 ✉ Via Lazzaretto 8, 20124 ☎ 02 2951 0837 ⏰ Wed–Mon lunch, dinner 🚇 Repubblica, Porta Venezia

SOLFERINO (€€)

www.ilsolferino.com

One of the oldest restaurants in the city, which serves excellent Milanese dishes in beautiful surroundings. The interior was completely overhauled in 2006. Meat and fish dishes are to the fore, but there are also good choices for vegetarians.

H3 ✉ Via Castelfidardo 2, 20121 ☎ 02 2900 5748 ⏰ Daily lunch, dinner 🚇 Moscova

TRANSATLANTICO (€)

Well-cooked pizza in this well-known art nouveau pizzeria. Try one of the unusual combinations, such as pizza stuffed with mussels and squid.

K3 ✉ Via Malpighi Marcello 3, 20129 ☎ 02 2952 6098 ⏰ Wed–Mon 🚇 Porta Venezia

Here is the heart of historic Milan and the meeting place for tourists and locals alike. The Piazza Duomo is dominated by the splendid wedding-cake of a cathedral, the third-largest in the world.

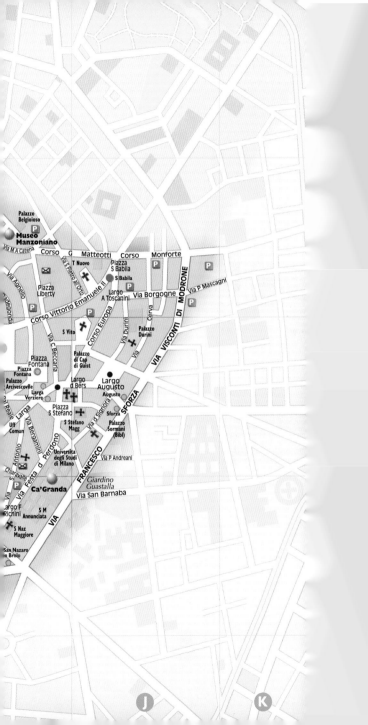

Palazzo
Belgioioso

**Museo
Manzoniano**

Via M.A.Catena

Corso G Matteotti Corso Monforte

T Nuovo

Piazza
Liberty

Via S Pietro all orto

Piazza
S Babila

S Babila

Largo
A Toscanini Via Borgogne

Corso Vittorio Emanuele II

Via Agnello

Via Cadegonda

Via C Ceccaria

Corso Europa

S Vito

Via Durini

Cerva

Palazzo
Durini

VIA VISCONTI DI MODRONE

Via P Mascagni

Palazzo
di Cap
di Guist

Piazza
Fontana

Piazza
Fontana

Palazzo
Arcivescovile

Largo
Verziere

Via Reale

Via Larga

Largo
d Bers

Largo
Augusto

Augusto

Via Bergamini

Piazza
S Stefano

S Stefano
Magg

Via d Signoria

SFORZA

Sforza

Palazzo
Sormani
(Bibl)

Uff
Comun

Via Antonio

Via Chiaravalle

Via Festa d Perdono

Universita
degli Studi
di Milano

FRANCESCO

Via P Andreani

Largo F
Richini

Ca'Granda

Giardino
Guastalla
Via San Barnaba

VIA

S M
Annunciata

S Naz
Maggiore

San Nazaro
in Brolo

J K

Ca' Granda

HIGHLIGHTS

● Cortile Maggiore—the spacious and elegant main courtyard with arcades surrounding the garden
● Fine 15th-century façade

This huge building certainly lives up to its name—Casa Grande or Large House. It houses the Humanities Department of the State University and retains elegant 15th-century courtyards and the lovely baroque Cortile Maggiore (Great Court).

Milan's benefactor Otherwise known as the Ospedale Maggiore, the building was commissioned by Francesco Sforza in the mid-15th century as the main hospital in Milan, which it remained for nearly five centuries. The plans of his architect, Filarete, were based on a rectangle made up of 10 equal squares with a church in the middle. Although Filarete's designs defined the entire building, only the right wing was constructed under the Sforzas. Guiniforte Solari (1429–91) completed Filarete's Renaissance section with the upper floor

Detail of a statue on Milan's Ca' Grande (far left). Statues flank the entrance (left). The beautiful arcaded building and courtyard (bottom far left). Students gather outside the historic casa (bottom middle). More striking columns and arcades (bottom right). The elaborate window ornamentation (below)

in Gothic style. In 1624, Francesco Maria Richini enlarged the hospital, and in 1797 the left wing was added. Ca' Granda was badly damaged by bombing in 1943, and owes its present-day look to postwar reconstruction and restoration, when it was converted to house the university.

Elegant but practical The lengthy façade (282m/925ft) illustrates the different stages of construction from the 15th century (on the far right) through to the late 18th century. The main courtyard is the Cortile Maggiore, with the Basilica dell'Annunciata opposite the entrance, and to the right are other elegant 15th-century courtyards. The hospital was very progressive for its day: men and women were separated, sanitary services were in corridors, and the beds had built-in cupboards and folding tables.

THE BASICS

www.unimi.it
✚ H7
✉ Via Festa del Perdono 5, 20122
☎ 02 503 111
🕐 Mon–Fri 8–6, Sat 8–12.30. Closed Aug
🍴 Basic student canteen
Ⓜ Missori
🚌 65, 77, 94; tram 12, 15
♿ Good
🖐 Free
ℹ No information or booklets

Duomo

HIGHLIGHTS

- The roof and the view
- The apse
- Stained-glass windows
- Trivulzio Candelabra (12th-century, crafted in gold)
- Treasury's collection of gold and silverwork
- The elaborate Crypt

TIP

- Be prepared for some scaffolding on the cathedral as ongoing restoration work is in progress. The present work is due to finish in 2007.

Symbol of the city, the sumptuous Duomo, with its huge proportions, towers over the Piazza Duomo. An ascent to the roof reveals a wonderful panorama of Milan and beyond.

Dazzling and ethereal The Duomo bristles with Gothic statues, gargoyles, pinnacles and soaring spires and has attracted comments from the censorious 'an imitation hedgehog' (D.H. Lawrence) to the lyrical 'a poem of marble' (Mark Twain). Ascend to the roof, by steps or elevator, for a wonderful panorama of Milan and, on a clear day, a view as far as the Alps.

Controversial building Milan's Duomo was founded in 1386 under the ambitious Gian Galeazzo Visconti, who resolved to build the

Soaring skyward—the elaborate towers of Milan's extraordinary cathedral (far left). Dominating the Piazza Duomo (middle). Feeding the many pigeons in the piazza (right). Singing angel sculpture adorns the façade of the Duomo (bottom left). More exquisite ornamentation (bottom middle). Intricate stonework (bottom right)

biggest church in Italy. Although the church was consecrated in 1418, it remained incomplete for over four centuries. Work finally started on the façade in the early 17th century, but was only finished in 1812, under Napoleon.

Into the darkness The Duomo is 157m (515ft) long, 33m (108ft) wide across the nave and 92m (302ft) wide across the transept; the roof is decorated with 2,245 statues, 135 spires and 96 gargoyles; the interior can hold 40,000 people. It is topped by the Madonnina, (the little Madonna), a gilded copper statue hoisted up here in 1774. After the stunning white exterior, the interior feels gloomy, but in the darkness your eye is drawn to the lively stained-glass windows. Monuments include the extraordinary statue of *The Flayed San Bartolomeo* (1562), with his skin draped over his shoulders.

THE BASICS

www.duomomilano.it

✚ H6

✉ Piazza del Duomo, 20121

☎ 02 8646 3456

🕐 Opening times: Cathedral daily 7–7. Treasury and crypt: daily 9.30–6. Baptistery: daily 9.30–5. Roof: Mar–end Oct daily 9.30–5.30; Nov–end Feb 9.30–4.15

Ⓜ Duomo

🚊 Tram 1, 2, 3, 15, 24 and others

♿ Main cathedral good. Crypt and Treasury not accessible

💵 Cathedral free. Roof entrance steps and elevator moderate. Treasury moderate

Galleria Vittorio Emanuele II

The Galleria is perfect for a stroll, window shop or pause for a sophisticated break

Linking Piazza del Duomo and Piazza della Scala, this elegant glass-roofed arcade has long been a popular rendezvous for the Milanese. It's worth indulging in a pricey cappuccino to watch the perpetual parade of stylish locals.

City reconstruction It was in 1865, after Unification, that the architect Giuseppe Mengoni offered his silver trowel to King Vittorio Emanuele II–after whom the arcade was named–to lay the foundation stone of the Galleria. Sadly, Mengoni fell to his death from the scaffolding a few days before the inauguration in 1897. The project's completion, in 1898, was marked by building a triumphal arch at the Duomo end. The creation of the arcade and the colossal demolition process that it involved reshaped the whole structure of the city.

Glitzy Milan This is a great place for shopping, eating and drinking–if you can afford it. The glass roof gives the arcade a feeling of light and space, even on a dull day. There are excellent bookshops, music stores and leather and clothes boutiques. A focal point is the central octagon area, under the glass dome, 47m (154ft) high. Pavement mosaics depict the coats of arms of the Savoy family and the symbols of Italian cities: Milan (red cross on a white background), Turin (a bull), Florence (a lily) and Rome (a she-wolf). Milanese tradition has it that stepping on the genitalia of the bull will bring you good luck. Savini (▷ 60), one of Milan's finest restaurants, is traditionally the meeting place of opera fans after first nights at La Scala.

The exterior of the Palazzo Reale, where banners advertise the temporary exhibitions

Palazzo Reale

In the heart of the city, beside (and inevitably dwarfed by) the Duomo, this historic palace was seat of the city council in the 11th century, ducal residence of the Viscontis and Sforzas, and the royal palace of the Austrian rulers.

A plethora of museums The Palazzo has been rebuilt several times, the present-day building owing its neoclassical appearance to the 1770s redevelopment of the square. It is worth a visit to see several beautifully restored rooms, and the Museo della Reggia, the pre-1990 works from the Civico Museo d'Arte Contemporanea (CIMAC) Contemporary Art collection, and for the major topical art exhibitions that are held here.

History of art The 11th-century Palazzo Broletto Vecchio (Courthouse) was rebuilt by the ruling Viscontis between 1330 and 1336, and redesigned in the 16th century by the Sforzas. Mozart performed at the theatre here in 1770, when he was 14. In the following decade the palace was rebuilt by Giuseppe Piermarini. Large sections of the palace were demolished in the 1920s and 1930s, and most of its dazzling interior was destroyed in the bombings of 1943. In the 1960s, the city bought the palace for use as museums, offices and to display art exhibitions. CIMAC was housed here in 1983 and has a fine collection of paintings with works by Picasso and Matisse. The first-floor Museo della Reggia has Gobelin tapestries and frescoes. The Museo del Duomo, which charts the history of the cathedral, is closed at the time of writing.

THE BASICS

➕ H6
✉ Piazza del Duomo 12, 20122
☎ 02 860 165
🕐 Tue–Sun 9.30–5.30, depending on exhibitions. Closed 1 Jan, Easter, 25 April, 1 May, 15 Aug, Christmas
🚇 Duomo
🚋 Tram 2, 3, 14, 15, 19, 24 and others
♿ Good
💶 Museo della Reggia free. Temporary exhibition prices vary.
ℹ Palazzo Reale bookshop for temporary exhibitions only. Museo del Duomo closed at time of writing; check with tourist office for new opening times

HIGHLIGHTS

● Museo della Reggia
● Freshly restored private apartments
● Films and concerts in the palace courtyards during the summer months

Piazza Mercanti

Locals and visitors alike gather at the attractive Piazza Mercanti

THE BASICS

🔲 G5
✉ Piazza Mercanti, 20123
🚇 Duomo
🚊 Tram 2, 3, 14, 15, 24
🍴 Al Mercante (café with outdoor tables, ▷ 59)

HIGHLIGHTS

● Loggia degli Orsi
● Palazzo delle Scuole Palatine (1645), a baroque palace with sculptures of St. Augustine and the Latin poet Ausonius
● Palazzo Panigarola, a handsome building with Gothic ogee arches

For centuries the administrative and commercial hub of the city, this central market square is rich in architecture and history. Rather more intimate than most piazzas in Milan, it is traffic-free and preserves its medieval character.

Origins The first buildings in this piazza were established in the 13th century and the square was enclosed by six gates, accessible only to the citizens of the quarter. The Palazzo della Ragione, built between 1228 and 1233 (▷ 54), served as the city's law courts for over five centuries, and its loggia was used for medieval market stalls.

Intimate appeal The piazza used to be much bigger, stretching to the far side of the present-day Via Mercanti, the wide pedestrian thoroughfare. On the north side is the huge Palazzo dei Giureconsulti, which houses the Chamber of Commerce. The Loggia degli Orsi, facing the Palazzo della Ragione, is a lovely pink-and-grey marble building that immediately draws the eye. The ground-floor arcade, now a bank, was used as a market. The coats of arms above are those of patrician families who lived in the quarter. Today, the piazza is a popular rendezvous, a pleasant spot for browsing in *bouquinistes* or lunching alfresco. The central well, with two Ionic columns supporting a pediment, dates from the 16th century. Unlike the nearby Piazza del Duomo, which is large and impersonal, the Piazza Mercanti has retained its intimate charm and even McDonald's at the east end manages to keep a low profile.

Basket of Fruit *by Caravaggio, displayed in the Pinocoteca Ambrosiana*

Pinacoteca Ambrosiana

THE BASICS

www.ambrosiana.it

⊞ G6

✉ Piazza Pio X1, 20123

☎ 02 806 921

🕐 Tue–Sun 10–5.30 (ticket office closes 4.30)

Ⓜ Cordusio, Duomo

🚊 Tram 2, 3, 14, 19, 24

♿ Good

💷 Expensive

🛈 Guidebooks and catalogues; shop sells good art books

HIGHLIGHTS

● Room 1: *Adoration of the Magi*, Titian

● Room 2: *The Musician*, Leonardo da Vinci

● Room 5: Raphael's cartoon for the *School of Athens* (1510), representing the greatest philosophers and mathematicians in conference

● Room 5: Caravaggio's staggeringly realistic *Basket of Fruit* (1594)

Cardinal Federico Borromeo built the Palazzo Ambrosiana in 1608 to house his collection of books and manuscripts. The art collection includes outstanding works by 15th- and 16th-century Italian and Flemish masters.

Phenomenal collection In the early 17th century, Cardinal Federico Borromeo commissioned eight experts to travel through Europe and the Middle East to amass a collection for his library. The Biblioteca Ambrosiana was set up with around 30,000 prints and 14,000 manuscripts. Nine years later, his personal collection of 127 paintings was added to form the Pinacoteca Ambrosiana. The building was extended in the 19th century, and today is run by a private and autonomous ecclesiastical foundation. From 1990 to 1997 the gallery closed for radical restructure; 10 new rooms were made accessible, enabling around 400 paintings to be displayed. Works by Leonardo, Titian, Raphael and Caravaggio are among those exhibited.

Essential viewing The ground-floor library has over 1,000 pages of drawings by Leonardo da Vinci—only accessible to scholars. On the first floor, rooms 1 and 4–7 display the Borromeo collection: Tuscan, Lombard and Venetian Renaissance and 17th-century Flemish art. The drawings displayed under glass are Leonardo reproductions. Rooms 2 and 3 display Renaissance masterpieces. Rooms 8–24 have 16th- to 20th-century paintings, sculpture and *objets d'art*, culminating in Manfredo Settala's diverse scientific collection.

Teatro alla Scala

Italy's premier opera house, built by Giuseppe Piermarini in the 18th century

THE BASICS

www.teatroallascala.org

✚ H5

✉ Piazza della Scala, 20121

☎ La Scala Information Point and La Scala Bookstore (Piazza della Scala 5) 02 869 2260

🎭 Opera season opening night always 7 Dec, feast day of Sant'Ambrogio, patron saint of Milan

🚇 Duomo, Cordusio

🚌 61; tram 1, 2

💶 Price depends on performance; museum moderate Good

DID YOU KNOW?

● The opera house has exceptionally fine acoustics.
● The stage is one of the largest in the world, measuring 1,200sq m (4,300sq ft).
● Most of the world's best-known conductors and opera singers have performed here.
● Tickets are notoriously hard to get, so book well in advance (performances sell out months in advance).

The world-famous La Scala, commisoned by Empress Maria Theresa of Austria, has seen the premières of many great classical Italian operas. The façade on Piazza della Scala is surprisingly sober, and belies the sumptuous auditorium.

Major overhaul The opera house, closed in 2002 for a major revamp, reopened for the 2004/2005 opera season to great acclaim.

World famous The opera house takes its name from the Santa Maria della Scala, the church on whose site it was built in 1776–78. It was built by Giuseppe Piermarini, architect of the Palazzo Reale, and took the place of the smaller Regio Ducale Teatro, which had been destroyed by fire. After the 1943 bombings, La Scala was the first of the city's monuments to be rebuilt. It reopened in 1946 and was re-inaugurated by Toscanini. The former artistic director came back from America after 17 years, having fled from Fascist Italy in 1929. Musical works by Rossini, Donizetti, Bellini, Verdi and Puccini had their debuts here, not always to great acclaim—the first night of Puccini's Madame Butterfly in 1904 was a complete fiasco—no one liked it!

Sumptuous interior The plush auditorium is decorated in red velvet and gilded stuccowork, with a 365-lamp crystal chandelier; it has an overall seating capacity of 2,015. You can view the auditorium as part of a museum tour. The Museo Teatrale alla Scala (▷ 54) contains a huge collection of theatrical memorabilia among its interesting exhibits.

More to See

CORSO DI PORTA ROMANA

The ancient route to Rome started at the Porta Romana (Roman Gate). One of the city's busiest streets, it is lined with small shops, pastisserie and cafés. The buildings of architectural interest, neoclassical and flamboyant art nouveau *palazzi*, lie toward the Piazza Missori end.

🞢 H7 ✉ 20121 🚇 Missori, Crocetta, Porta Romana 🚌 77; tram 24

MUSEO MANZONIANO

www.museidelcentro.mi.it

Overlooking Piazza Belgioioso in the heart of the city, this was the home of Alessandro Manzoni, considered the greatest Italian novelist of the 19th century. Born in Milan, he lived here almost continuously, from 1814 until he died in 1873. You can visit his study, library, the living rooms, 'the wedding bedroom' and the bedroom where he died.

🞢 H5 ✉ Via G. Morone 1 (Piazza Belgioioso), 20121 ☎ 02 8646 60403 🕐 Tue–Fri, Sun 9–12, 2–4 🚇 Duomo 🚌 61; tram 1, 2 🚹 Good 🖢 Free

MUSEO TEATRALE ALLA SCALA

The museum was founded in 1913 and has a superb collection of theatrical memorabilia. This ranges from ornate stage-curtain design, antique musical instruments, phonographs and gramophones, sketches for sets, costumes (including those for Maria Callas and Rudolf Nureyev) and the Sambon collection of paintings and ceramics. You can take a tour of the auditorium, too.

🞢 G5 ✉ Piazza della Scala, 20121 ☎ 02 8879 7473 🕐 Daily 9–12.30, 1.30–5.30, last visit 5. Closed 1 Jan, 1 May, 15 Aug, 25–26 Dec 🚇 Duomo, Cordusio 🚌 61, tram 1, 2 🚹 Good 🖢 Moderate

PALAZZO DELLA RAGIONE

A splendid redbrick medieval building, with rounded arches and a ground-floor loggia that dominates Piazza Mercanti (▷ 50). It was built in 1233 by the *podestà* (governor), Oldrado da Tresseno, who is depicted in an equestrian relief on the side facing the square.

🞢 G6 ✉ Piazza Mercanti, 20123 🕐 View from outside only 🚇 Duomo 🚌 Tram 2, 3, 15, 24

Splendid statue on the façade of the Palazzo della Ragione

PALAZZO MARINO

On the same square as the Teatro alla Scala, this is an imposing baroque palace with a late-19th-century façade. It was built in 1558 for Tommaso Marino, a wealthy Genoese financier, and since 1860 it has been the city's Town Hall. The palace is not open to the public, but don't miss the porticoed Courtyard of Honour, which can be glimpsed from Via Marina (to the right as you face the façade).

🚻 H5 ✉ Piazza della Scala, 20121 🕐 View from outside only 🚇 Duomo, Cordusio 🚌 61; tram 1, 2

SAN FEDELE

This church is one of the city's finest examples of baroque architecture. The elaborate façade is decorated with reliefs on the pediment and sculpted figures in the niches. Although internally less exciting, the church has some beautifully carved wooden furniture.

🚻 H5 ✉ Piazza Fedele, 20121 ☎ No phone 🕐 Daily 7.30–2.30, 4–7 🚇 Duomo 🚌 61; tram 1, 2 ♿ Poor; 7 steps up to church 🚻 Free

SANTA MARIA PRESSO SAN SATIRO

This gem of a church is squeezed between four streets southwest of the Duomo. The original ninth-century building was brilliantly restructured by Donato Bramante, who created the illusion of depth by using gilded stucco and *trompe l'oeil*.

🚻 G6 ✉ Via Speronari 3, 20123, entrance on Via Torino ☎ 02 7202 1804 🕐 Mon–Fri 7.30–11.30, 3.30–6.30; Sat, Sun, public holidays 9–12, 3.15–6.45 🚇 Duomo 🚌 Tram 2, 3, 14, 15, 16, 24 ♿ Poor 🚻 Free

VIA DANTE

Linking Largo Cairoli to Castello Sforzesco, this pedestrian thoroughfare was built at the end of the 19th century. Alfresco cafés spill out onto the street, and elegant shops occupy the lower floors of fine neoclassical buildings. The northwest end of the street is dominated by an equestrian statue of Garibaldi and beyond it is the soaring clock tower of the Castello.

🚻 G5 ✉ 20121 🚇 Cordusio, Cairoli 🚌 18, 50, 58; tram 19, 24 and others

Santa Maria Presso San Satiro church

Eating alfresco on the Via Dante

City Highlights

This stroll through the heart of Milan will introduce you to some of the city's most famous landmarks.

DISTANCE: 2km (1.25 miles) **ALLOW:** 2 hours plus stops

START

PIAZZA DEL DUOMO
✚ H6 Ⓜ Duomo

END

PIAZZA DEL DUOMO
✚ H6 Ⓜ Duomo

❶ Start at the Piazza del Duomo, dominated by the west front of the Duomo (▷ 46–47). Walk along the right side of the cathedral and turn right down the narrow Via Palazzo Reale.

❷ Pass between Palazzo Reale (▷ 49) and Palazzo Arcivescovile. Go round the back of the palace via the bell tower and the rotunda. Turn left at the end of Via delle Ore.

❸ Enter Piazza Fontana, with the 1783 fountain by Piermarini. Look behind it for a fine view of the Duomo and then return to the Piazza del Duomo.

❹ Turn right through Galleria Vittorio (▷ 48) into Piazza della Scala. Cross in front of the Palazzo Marino and turn right. Take another right behind the *palazzo*.

❽ Passing in front of La Scala, follow Via Santa Margherita down to Piazza Mercanti (▷ 50), into Via Mercanti, which leads back to the Duomo.

❼ Now in Piazza Belgioioso you can find Manzoni's house, now the Museo Manzoniano (▷ 54). Continue to Via Manzoni, where Museo Poldi Pezzoli (▷ 26) is on the right. Turn left back into Piazza della Scala, with the opera house, La Scala (▷ 52), on your right.

❻ Here, too is the statue of writer Manzoni. Leaving the piazza the way you entered, walk alongside the church. You will see Casa degli Omenoni ahead on the left, once home to the sculptor Leone Leoni.

❺ This brings you into the Piazza San Fedele, with its baroque church.

WALK

CENTRO STORICO

Shopping

ALESSI
www.alessi.com
Alessi has everything for the home and office. Drinks accessories, from wine coolers to cork-screws, and a host of containers, textiles, trays and items for children's rooms.
📍 J5 ✉ Corso Matteotti 9, 20121 ☎ 02 795 726 🚇 San Babila

ANDREW'S TIES
www.andrewsties.com
Italian ties made of wool, silk and cashmere in every imaginable shade and design. Shirts and sweaters as well.
📍 H5 ✉ Galleria Vittorio Emanuele II, 20121 ☎ 02 860 935 🚇 Duomo

BORSALINO
Milan's oldest milliners should be the first port of call if you are looking to buy a hat.
📍 H5 ✉ Galleria Vittorio Emanuele II, 20121 ☎ 02 8901 5436 🚇 Duomo

DISCOVERY
Browse through rare vinyl albums by the Beatles, Lou Reed and Jimi Hendrix, all priced around €8. Picture discs cost slightly more.
📍 G6 ✉ Passaggio Santa Margherita (just off Piazza Mercanti), 20123 ☎ 339 699 9417; e-mail matteo.ceshi@ tiscali.it 🚇 Duomo

FURLA
www.furla.com
Chic leather bags and belts in high-fashion,

minimalist designs, but with an original twist. Also scarves and shoes. Affordable prices.
📍 H5 ✉ Corso Vittorio Emanuele II (corner of Piazza Liberty), 20122 ☎ 02 796 943 🚇 San Babila

GARBAGNATI
The most famous bakery in Milan, especially renowned for its delicious *panettone*.
📍 G5 ✉ Via Victor Hugo 3, 20123 ☎ 02 860 905 🚇 Duomo

GIOVANNI GALLI
www.giovannigalli.com
The shop for those who love all things sweet. The marrons glacés are legendary, and the traditional

DEPARTMENT STORES
Department stores are still rather alien to most Italians and Milan has only a handful. The best department store is La Rinascente (📍 H5 ✉ Via Radegonda 3 ☎ 02 88 521), a monumental shop opposite the Duomo. It stretches over six floors and sells almost everything you could possibly want. Coin (📍 K6 ✉ Piazza Cinque Giornate 1/a ☎ 02 5519 2083) is also good, and sells a full range of quality products. More downmarket, Upim Duomo (📍 G6 ✉ Via Torino/Via Spadari ☎ 02 8901 0750) sells most items at really low prices.

sweets and biscuits are good, too.
📍 H7 ✉ Corso di Porta Romana 2, 20122 ☎ 02 8645 3112 🚇 Missori

LIBRERIA HOEPLI
www.hoepli.it
Established in 1870, this bookshop, extending over six floors, has the most extensive stock in Milan of books in any language, on any subject.
📍 H5 ✉ Via Hoepli 5, 20121 ☎ 02 864 871 🚇 Duomo

MANDARINA DUCK
www.mandarinaduck.com
On two floors, one of Italy's leading luggage stores, trading on a stunning blend of style and function.
📍 G6 ✉ Via Orefici 10, 20123 ☎ 02 8646 2198 🚇 Cordusio

PAPIER
A delightful stationers selling handcrafted items made from natural, undyed paper and paper produced using coconut, cotton and silk.
📍 G6 ✉ Via San Maurillo 4, 20123 ☎ 02 865 221 🚇 Duomo, Cordusio

PECK
www.peck.it
Probably Milan's most prestigious delicatessen, with numerous different stalls specializing in bread, cheese, seafood, salami, marinated vegetables and Mediterranean delights.
📍 G6 ✉ Via Spadari 9, 20121 ☎ 02 8023161 🚇 Duomo

POLLINI

Up-to-the-minute boots and bags for men and women in lively styles.
✚ J5 ✉ Corso Vittorio Emanuele II 30, 20122 ☎ 02 794 912 Ⓜ San Babila

PRADA

www.furla.com
The outside of this flagship branch of Prada has graced a thousand fashion photographs, and the window display is second to none.
✚ H5 ✉ Galleria Vittorio Emanuele II 63, 20122 ☎ 02 876 979 Ⓜ San Babila

RICORDI MEGASTORE

www.lafeltrinelli.it
One of Italy's best music stores and the first of its kind in Milan, selling books on composers and their works, recorded music and sheet music, plus instruments. Also, concert tickets available.
✚ H5 ✉ Galleria Vittorio Emanuele II, 20121 ☎ 02 8646 0272 Ⓜ Duomo

SISLEY

www.sisley.com
This Italian designer's window displays draw the shoppers in droves. Quality Italian men's shirts, ladies' T-shirts and the latest lingerie. Also a whole floor devoted to things for the home.
✚ H6 ✉ Via Dogana 4, 20123 ☎ 02 8050 9415 Ⓜ Duomo

Entertainment and Nightlife

LA BANQUE

www.labanque.it
A popular nightspot in a former bank. A range of music fills the dance floor, which was once the bank's vault. Happy hour at 6pm weekdays.
✚ G5 ✉ Via E. Porrone 6, 20121 ☎ 02 8699 6565 Ⓜ Cordusio

ODEON

A huge mainstream cinema in the middle of Milan showing the latest American blockbusters, many in their original language, so you can still catch the latest releases from home. This 10-screen complex has good access for visitors with disabilities.
✚ H5 ✉ Via Santa Radegonda 8, 20121 ☎ 02 874 547 Ⓜ Duomo

TEATRO ALLA SCALA

www.teatroallascala.org
Opera, classical and the occasional musical boom out from Milan's, and possibly the world's, most prestigious playhouse. It's not just famous names at La Scala; Maria Callas was unknown when she made her debut here. The venue has a bar, museum, visitor area and an excellent bookshop with many titles in English.
✚ H5 ✉ Piazza della Scala, 20121 ☎ 02 7200 3744 Ⓜ Montenapoleone

THE BIG SCREEN

Going to the cinema is a popular pastime for the Milanese and there are a number of cinemas close to the heart of the city. There are also many multiplexes farther out: Arcadia (☎ 02 9541 6445), 28km (18 miles) east of the city at Melzo, is part of a huge site with shops and restaurants, and houses Energia, the biggest screen in Italy.

TEATRO NUOVO

www.teatronouvo.it
All types of theatre are staged here, including some excellent comedy, musicals and dance productions. There is capacity for over 1,000 people, who come to see performances by some of the famous actors who appear here on a regular basis.
✚ J5 ✉ Piazza San Babila, 20121 ☎ 02 7600 0086 Ⓜ San Babila

Restaurants

PRICES

Prices are approximate, based on a 3-course meal for one person.

€€€	over €50
€€	€20–€50
€	under €20

AL MERCANTE (€€)

www.ristorantealmercante.it
Eat outside in summer at this restaurant in one of the most attractive medieval squares in Milan. Tasty pasta, meat and fish dishes, and a good wine list.

➕ G6 ✉ Piazza Mercanti 17, 20123 ☎ 02 805 2198 🕐 Mon–Sat lunch, dinner 🚇 Duomo, Cordusio

CAFFÈ MARTINI (€)

At this café/bar, seating is either in the upper balcony area, with mirrors and chandeliers, or outside under canopies with heaters. Good snacks such as *panini* and salads.

➕ G6 ✉ Via dei Mercanti 21, 20123 ☎ 02 7200 0366 🕐 Daily 6–1 🚇 Cordusio

CAFFÈ REAL (€–€€€)

www.caferealmilano.it
This is one of a number of relaxing, chic, lounge restaurants popular in Milan. Light bites and coffees by day and international and Italian cuisine by night. Also hosts themed music evenings.

➕ J6 ✉ Via Merlo 21, 20121 ☎ 02 7631 6505 🕐 Daily 7–3, 8–11 (kitchen from 12) 🚇 Duomo, San Babila

CAFFÈ SFORZESCO (€)

A pleasant place for an alfresco drink or lunch after sightseeing at the Duomo or a hard morning shopping, before an afternoon of relaxing in the park or visiting the castle.

➕ G5 ✉ Via dei Meravigli 2, 20123 ☎ 02 8055 5016 🕐 Daily 🚇 Cordusio

CHARLESTON (€)

In the heart of the shopping and theatre area, serving a wide variety of pizza plus some interesting Florentine dishes. Dine under the gazebo in summer.

➕ H5 ✉ Piazza del Liberty 8, 20121 ☎ 02 798 631

A PLETHORA OF PIZZA

There's pizza and there's pizza. Every city in the world produces this famous Italian dish but it never tastes the same as in the country of its birth and you will find some of the best in Milan. Seek out the pizzerias where the food is cooked in the traditional manner in wood-fired ovens (*forno a legna*). They are usually thin crust and made from age-old recipes, and the best ones are normally prepared by one of the many Neapolitan chefs working in the city. A true Italian pizza does not include exotic toppings such as pineapple or sweetcorn.

🕐 Daily 🚇 Duomo, San Babila

CRACCO-PECK (€€€)

www.cracco-peck.it
Modern Italian cuisine cooked with the finest and freshest ingredients have given Carlo Cracco's restaurant an international reputation. Reservations advised.

➕ H5 ✉ Via Victor Hugo 4, 20123 ☎ 02 876 774 🕐 Mon–Fri lunch, dinner; Sat dinner only. Closed 2 weeks Aug 🚇 Duomo

DAI DAMM (€)

Excellent spot for lunch and a rest from sightseeing, or for after-show pizza and good fish dishes.

➕ G6 ✉ Via Torino 34, 20123 ☎ 02 8645 3482 🕐 Tue–Sun all day; Mon lunch only 🚇 Duomo

DI GENNARO (€)

Not far from the Duomo and good for an after-show meal, this pizzeria has been producing classics from the old-fashioned tiled oven for many years.

➕ H5 ✉ Via Santa Radegonda 14, 20121 ☎ 02 805 3454 🕐 Fri–Wed all day 🚇 Duomo

IL GABBIANO (€)

Near the Duomo, this *gelateria* sells milk shakes and fruit salad as well as a large selection of ice cream and sorbets. You can also sit outside.

➕ H5 ✉ Via Ugo Foscolo 3, 20121 ☎ 02 7202 2411 🕐 Daily 🚇 Duomo

MARCHESI (€)

Enjoy the pastries, tarts, salads and much more at this Milan institution. Take away some sweets, cakes or chocolates—the gift-wrapping is a joy.

🚩 F5 ✉ Via Santa Maria alla Porta 11a, 20123 ☎ 02 876 730 🕐 Mon–Sat 7.30am–8pm, Sun 8.30–1 Ⓜ Cordusio, Cairoli

IL ROSA AL CAMINETTO (€€)

www.ilrosa.it

Just a stone's throw from the Duomo, this intimate restaurant is perfectly placed for quick lunches or lingering romantic dinners. It also caters for those with children and there is even a playroom. Traditional main courses are followed by tempting desserts from the hand of the pastry chef. Good wines, too.

🚩 H6 ✉ Via Cesare Beccaria 4, 20120 ☎ 02 8909 5235 🕐 Daily lunch, dinner Ⓜ Duomo

SANT'AMBROEUS (€€)

The ultimate pastry shop that oozes class. Wonderful window displays get the taste buds going. Beautiful tea room and tables outside.

🚩 J5 ✉ Corso Matteotti 7, 20121 ☎ 02 7600 0540 🕐 Daily, closed 3 weeks Aug Ⓜ San Babila

SAVINI (€€€)

www.thi.it/savini

Legendary Milanese restaurant that has been serving food since 1867,

especially to the rich and famous visiting Teatro alla Scala. The well-prepared food, based on the finest ingredients, lives up to the best Milanese traditions.

🚩 H5 ✉ Galleria Vittorio Emanuele II, 20121 ☎ 02 7200 3433 🕐 Daily lunch, dinner. Closed 3 weeks Aug Ⓜ Duomo

TANDUR (€€)

www.ristorantetandur.com

First-class Indian fare right in the *centro storico*. Tandur specializes in tandoori dishes.

🚩 G6 ✉ Via Maddalena 3, 20122 ☎ 02 805 6192 🕐 Tue–Sat lunch, dinner, Sun dinner Ⓜ Missori

TRATTORIA MILANESE (€)

For a taste of old Milan, come to this tiny trattoria in the heart of the city. In business for a century,

the trattoria reflects the past and the excellent food lives up to the Milanese tradition.

🚩 G6 ✉ Via Santa Marta 11, 20123 ☎ 02 8645 1991 🕐 Wed–Mon lunch, dinner Ⓜ Cordusio, Missori

VICTORIA CAFFÈ (€€)

www.victoriacaffe.it

Discreet café behind the Piazza della Scala; the perfect spot for a pizza or pasta lunch, an early-evening drink or after dinner nightcap.

🚩 G5 ✉ Via Clerici 1, 20121 ☎ 02 805 3598/869 0792 🕐 Daily Ⓜ Duomo

YAR (€€€)

Milan's only dedicated Russian restaurant. Pricey, but the fixed-price menu is less expensive. Dried smoked fish, *borsht* and deer steak.

🚩 H8 ✉ Via Mercalli Giuseppe 22, 20122 ☎ 02 5830 5234 🕐 Mon–Sat dinner only Ⓜ Missori

ZUCCA IN GALLERIA (€€)

www.caffemiani.it

Famous Milan bar, owned by the Miani family, with an outside terrace ideal for people-watching. Coffee, lunch or evening drink—the choice is yours but prepare to pay a high price.

🚩 H6 ✉ Piazza Duomo 21, 20121 ☎ 02 8646 4435 🕐 Tue–Sun. Closed Aug Ⓜ Duomo

Probably one of the most attractive parts of Milan, dominated by Parco Sempione and the austere Castello Sforzesco. In complete contrast, the bohemian Brera offers medieval streets, restaurants and bars.

Arco della Pace

TOP 25

Triumphal detail from the impressive Arco della Pace at the north end of Parco Sempione

THE BASICS

➕ E3

✉ Piazza Sempione, 20154 and 20145

🍴 Café

🚌 57, 61; tram 1, 30

♿ Good

HIGHLIGHTS

● The huge bronze Chariot of Peace (25m/82ft high)
● A distant view from the Parco Sempione
● The initial impact as you approach from Corso Sempione

Milan's triumphal arch was intended as a monument to Napoleon's victories. With his fall from power in 1814, the project came to a standstill and he was never to see its completion.

Napoleon's dream The Arch of Victories, as it was at first known, was finally finished in 1838 under the Austrian Emperor, Ferdinand I. In commemoration of the European Peace Treaty of 1815 he changed the name to the Arch of Peace (Arco della Pace) and made appropriate changes to the bas-reliefs. The formal monument marks the northwest end of the Parco Sempione, and the start of the Corso Sempione, Napoleon's highway to the Simplon Pass.

Monumental construction The arch was designed by Luigi Cagnola and inspired by the arch of Septimius Severus in the Forum in Rome. Work began in 1807, halted in 1814, and resumed in 1826 under Ferdinand I of Austria. The circular piazza around it was redesigned in the 1980s and closed to traffic. The arch is best seen from a distance, preferably from the park side, where you can see the Chariot of Peace on the top of the monument. A facelift has returned the arch to its former glory and the marble gleams once again.

Beyond the arch The two buildings either side of the arch on the park side were toll houses. Open-air concerts are held in the circular piazza on summer evenings, but otherwise the area is best avoided after dark.

Both inside and out you will find some first-class Roman objects in this museum

Civico Museo Archeologico

Milan was once a powerful Roman city and this museum, in the ruins of the Benedictine Maggiore monastery, exhibits some fine examples of Roman sculpture and everyday items.

Moving collections The exhibits were formerly housed in the Castello Sforzesco, in the city's archaeological and numismatic collections. Following World War II, several sections were transferred here, next to the church of San Maurizio, with some remaining in the Castello. The monastery, once the largest women's convent in Milan, was built in the ninth century, rebuilt in the early 16th, and was badly bombed in 1943.

Roman and other finds Fragments of Roman funerary stones, sarcophagi and capitals are arranged around the cloister at the front of the museum, with pride of place going to the Masso di Bormo, a large stone whose carvings date back to the third millennium BC. Inside, a model of Roman Milan (Mediolanum) introduces the Roman collection. The basement is devoted to Greek and Etruscan exhibits and a tiny section to works of art from Gandha-ra (what is now northern Pakistan and Afghanistan). Take a look at the Coppa Trivulzio in the Roman section, which is behind the black screen and quite easy to miss. It is an exquisite late fourth-century goblet in emerald-green glass, carved from a single piece of glass. The Roman Parabiago Plate is a large silver-gilt, embossed patera (weighing 3.5kg/8lb) discovered in 1907, from Parabiago, northwest of Milan.

THE BASICS

➕ F5
✉ Corso Magenta 15, 20123
☎ 02 8645 0011
🕐 Tue–Sun 9–1, 2–5.30 (last admission 5)
Ⓜ Cadorna, Cairoli
🚌 50, 58; tram 18, 19
♿ Poor; phone ahead
💶 Inexpensive, free Fri after 2
ℹ Small booklets in English, inexpensive

HIGHLIGHTS

● Coppa Trivulzio
● Parabiago Plate
● The torso of Hercules. It was discovered among ruins of Roman baths on what is now Corso Europa.
● *Portrait of Maximin* (mid-3rd-century AD); one of a series of portraits dating from Caesar's era.

Castello Sforzesco

HIGHLIGHTS

● Mausoleum of Bernabò Visconti (1363), Bonino da Campione

● Salle delle Asse, with fresco decoration attributed to Leonardo

● Sala degli Scarlioni: Michaelangelo's *Rondanini Pietà* (1554–64) and Gaston de Foix's funerary monument, *Agostini Busti*

TIP

● Lots to see–visit the museums on a wet day, the grounds on a sunny one.

A landmark of Milan, the castle is a vast brick quadrilateral, dominated on the town side by the Filarete Tower. It stands as a symbol of the Golden Renaissance Age, and today is home to the excellent civic museums.

Through the centuries Built as a fortress by the Visconti family between 1358 and 1368, the castle was all but demolished after their downfall. It was transformed into a Renaissance fort under Francesco Sforza, and his son, who became Duke of Milan, turned it into a sumptuous residence. By the early 19th century, Napoleon turned what was left of the building into soldiers' quarters. In 1884, the city planned a virtual demolition of the castle, but the architect Luca Beltrami transformed it into a museum.

Outer wall of the Castello Sforzesco (far left). Poster for an exhibition inside the castle (left). Bronze statuary displayed in the porticoed courtyard within the castle (right). Fountain in front of the castle (bottom left). Armoured soldier in the Musei del Castello (bottom middle left). Tourist entrance (bottom middle right). Castle statue (bottom right)

Exploring the museums Start your visit at the entrance under the Filarete Tower. Beyond the massive Piazza d'Armi is the Renaissance Corte Ducale, residence of the Sforzas, around which the Civiche Raccolte d'Arte Antica is displayed. This rich collection of sculpture spans 12 centuries, from a fourth-century sarcophagus to Michelangelo's *Rondanini*—the highlight of the whole collection. On the upper floor is the furniture collection and the Art Gallery, whose Italian Renaissance master-pieces include works by Mantegna, Giovanni Bellini, Antonella da Messina and Filippo Lippi, as well as a rich collection of works by Lombard artists. The first and second floors are devoted to the applied arts, which include an outstanding collection of musical instruments and the rare Trivulzio Tapestries, designed by Bramantino. The basement houses the Archaeology Museum.

THE BASICS

www.milanocastello.it

✚ F4

✉ Piazza Castello, 20121

☎ 02 8846 3703

🕐 Castello: daily summer 7–7, winter 7–6. Museums: Tue–Sun 9–5.30. Castle and museum closed 1 Jan, Easter, 1 May, 25 Dec

🚇 Cadorna, Cairoli, Lanza

🚌 57; tram 1, 4, 27

♿ Good; some steps

🎫 Moderate, free Fri after 2

ℹ Guidebooks available

Corso Magenta

Stroll down Corso Magenta and then take a coffee at the Caffè Litta (below)

THE BASICS

➕ D5–F5

✉ Extending east from Porta Magenta to the junction with Via Meravigli

🍴 Numerous cafés and restaurants

Ⓜ Conciliazione, Cadorna

🚌 18, 67; tram 16, 19

HIGHLIGHTS

● Santa Maria delle Grazie and Leonardo da Vinci's *The Last Supper* (c1495–97) (▷ 72–73)

● Civico Museo Archeologico (▷ 65)

● San Maurizio (▷ 71)

● Bar Magenta–historic café (▷ 77)

Any visit to Milan should include this *corso*, one of Milan's most elegant streets flanked by historic *palazzi* and home to Leonardo da Vinci's *The Last Supper* at the Church of Santa Maria delle Grazie.

Along the old road The oldest trace of civilization here is the Roman tower in the grounds of the Archaeological Museum (▷ 65), the only surviving above-ground section of the city's Roman walls. On the same site are the ruins of the ancient Benedictine Maggiore Monastery, founded in the ninth century and remodelled in the early 1500s. The rest of the Corso is more recent, typified by baroque, neoclassical and 19th-century mansions.

Plenty to see This is one of Milan's most affluent districts, a desirable residential and shopping area, with chic boutiques, antique shops and several historic buildings. The great magnet is the Church of Santa Maria delle Grazie, whose splendid terracotta bulk dominates this section of the Corso. The piazza is normally milling with visitors, awaiting their alloted 15-minute slot for da Vinci's *The Last Supper* in the Refectory adjoining the church. Going east, the Palazzo delle Stelline at No. 59, a school for orphans in the 17th century, has been transformed out of recognition into a conference facility and hotel. Beyond the crossroads, you can't miss the large baroque façade of Palazzo Litta (No. 24), now home to the Teatro Litta (▷ 77), and across the road, beyond the Archaeological Museum, the Church of San Maurizio (No. 15) is full of fabulous 16th-century frescoes.

FERROVIE DELLO STATO

S, A.

Parco Sempione

Cool and inviting, particularly in summer, the park is popular with locals and visitors

THE BASICS

✚ E3

✉ Piazza Castello–Piazza Sempione (8 entrances around perimeter)

☎ Torre Branca: 02 331 4120

🕐 Park: daily 6.30am–8/9/10/11.30pm depending on season. Torre Branca: Tue, Thu 9.30pm–1am; Wed 10.30–12.30, 4–6.30, 8.30–1; Sat, Sun 10.30–2, 2.30–7, 8.30–1. Winter hours are shorter; check before visiting. Closed in bad weather

🍴 Cafés in park

Ⓜ Cadorna, Cairioli, Lanza, Moscova

🚌 43, 57, 61, 94; tram 1, 4, 27

✋ Park free; Torre Branca moderate, over 60s and children under 3 free

HIGHLIGHTS

● Arena Civica
● Torre Branca
● *Bagni Misteriosi*, sculpture by Giorgio de Chirico, found behind the Palazzo dell'Arte
● View of Arco della Pace from the lake

A welcome break from the city noise, with a fine view of the Castello Sforzesco, the Parco Sempione was once part of the vast hunting ground of the Sforza family, who occupied the castle. It became a public park in the late 19th century.

Early uses In the early 1800s the French used the land as an exercise ground for their armed forces. Napoleon had plans to build a great piazza around the castle and turn the whole area into the new heart of the city, but apart from the Arco della Pace (▷ 64) and the Arena Civico (▷ 74) the plans never materialized. The public park, 47ha (116 acres) in size, was begun in 1893 when Emilio Alemagna landscaped the area on the lines of an English park—as was the fashion.

The country in town The gardens stretch from the castle to the Arco della Pace—a landscape of lawns, large trees, winding paths and a lake with a small bridge. On the west side, you can't miss the Torre Branca, an Eiffel Tower-like steel structure (1933) that's open after many years of closure. The designer Roberto Cavalli has opened a restaurant at the base of the tower (▷ 78). The nearby Palazzo dell'Arte was opened a year before the tower as a permanent site of the Triennale Decorative Arts Exhibition. The park is dotted with modern sculpture and monuments, and has lots for children, including sailing boats on the lake. The park is popular with locals and there's entertainment in the summer months. Although the park is open late into the evening, it is best avoided after dark.

Divine art—St. Luke the Evangelist attributed to Vincenzo Foppa

San Maurizio

THE BASICS

➕ F5
✉ Corso Magenta 15, 20123
🕐 Tue–Sun 9–1, 2.30–5.30 (can sometimes close for no reason); closed 1 Jan, 1 May, 25 Dec
Ⓜ Cadorna
🚌 50, 58; tram 18, 19
♿ Poor
🆓 Free
ℹ Guidebooks in Italian only

The unremarkable grey baroque façade of this church on the busy Corso Magenta gives no hint of the glorious interior. Step inside and you are greeted by a riot of beautiful baroque frescoes, decorating every surface.

HIGHLIGHTS

● Frescoes by Bernardino Luini, including *Life of St. Catherine*
● *The Adoration of the Magi*, Antonio Campi
● Frescoes by unattributed artists
● Classical concerts in the nuns' hall in winter
● Excellent lighting to view the frescoes in detail

Important convent The church was built in 1503 for the adjoining Monastero Maggiore, formerly one of the most prestigious monasteries in Milan, and home to Benedictine nuns. The monastery was largely destroyed in the 19th century but is today the site of the Civico Museo Archeologico (▷ 65). A schedule of restoration of the church frescoes has been ongoing since 1986.

Church meets state The church was constructed in two main parts: one hall for the congregation and a larger cloistered hall for the nuns. The two were separated by a partition wall and altar, which face you as you go into the church. The nuns were able to participate in Eucharist celebrated in the public hall through the little doors, which you can see in the arch in the central fresco to the left of the altar; they could also receive Communion through the tiny opening (the *comunichino*) on the right of the altar below the figure of Christ.

Wonderful frescoes On both sides of the partition wall is the *Passion of Christ*. Many of the frescoes were executed by Bernardino Luini (c1480–1532), one of the most prominent Lombard followers of Leonardo da Vinci; the chapels on the left were decorated by his pupils.

Santa Maria delle Grazie

HIGHLIGHTS

- *The Last Supper*, Leonardo da Vinci (in the adjoining Refectory)
- The Bramante Cloister
- Chapel of St. Corona, with frescoes by Guadenzio Ferrari
- *Crowning of Thorns*, Titian
- Madonna delle Grazie Chapel
- *Madonna delle Grazie delivering Milan from the Plague*, Il Cerano

TIPS

- It is not possible to view *The Last Supper* without reserving ahead.
- Book for early in the day.

While *The Last Supper* is a real highlight, the church itself should not be missed. Although it was built over a mere 26 years, it gives the impression of two completely different churches.

Renaissance gem Guiniforte Solari designed the church for the Dominican Order in 1463–90. The contrast of styles between the Dominican late-Gothic nave, with its wealth of decoration, and the pure, harmonious domed apse built by Bramante marks the rapid change that came with the Renaissance. In 1943, a bomb destroyed the cloister, but, miraculously, two of its greatest treasures, *The Last Supper* and the dome, survived.

Glorious architecture The magnificent brick and terracotta exterior, crowned by Bramante's grand

Detail from Leonardo da Vinci's The Last Supper *(left). Exterior view of Santa Maria della Grazie (middle). The fine marble and terracotta decoration on the church's dome (right). Ornamentation on the façade (bottom left). Overall view of the church (bottom middle). Detail of the arches at the top of the dome (bottom middle right)*

dome, is best seen from Corso Magenta. From the Renaissance portal, you enter Solari's nave, with its richly decorated arches and vaults. Beyond it, Bramante's apse feels simple in comparison. The beautiful Bramante Cloister, surrounding a garden, is familiarly known as Chiostrino delle Rane after the bronze frogs (*rane*) at the fountain. If a service is in progress, you can reach the cloister via the street entrance on Via Caradosso.

Da Vinci's masterpiece Ludovico Il Moro commissioned this fresco in the refectory adjoining the church in 1494, and it is one of the most famous in the world. Unfortunately the experimental techniques used by da Vinci led to signs of deterioration within 20 years of completing the work. Much restoration has been done to return the painting to its former glory. Booking in advance is compulsory.

THE BASICS

✚ E5
✉ Piazza Santa Maria delle Grazie, 20123
☎ 02 467 6111
🕐 Mon–Sat 6.50–12, 3–7; Sun, public holidays 7–12.30, 3.30–8.45 (no visits during services)
🚇 Conciliazione
🚌 18; tram 16
♿ Good; 3 steps
💵 Free; English guide to church and *The Last Supper* expensive
❓ You need to book at least 2 days in advance to view *The Last Supper*. Reservations ☎ 02 8942 1146

73

More to See

ACQUARIO

www.acquariocivicomi.it

Set in a fine art nouveau building, this excellent aquarium was completed in March 2006. It houses some 150 different species from both marine and freshwater environments. Check out the transparent 'bridge' tank so visitors can look at the fish from all angles.

➕ F4 ✉ Via Gadio 2, 20121 ☎ 02 8846 5750 🕐 Tue–Sun 9–1, 2–5.30 Ⓜ Lanza ♿ Good 🖐 Free at time of writing

ARENA CIVICO

This huge amphitheatre was built in 1806 by Luigi Canonica to seat 30,000 spectators. It has since hosted soccer games and pop concerts; today it is mainly used for athletic events.

➕ F3 ✉ North end of Via Legano, Via Comizi di Lione 1, Parco Sempione, 20154 🕐 Open for events only Ⓜ Lanza 🚌 57, 70; tram 3, 4, 12, 14

BRERA DISTRICT

The Brera is one of the oldest and most attractive districts in Milan. For many years this quarter was inhabited by artists and there is still a hint of Bohemia. Via Brera is its liveliest street, popular with the young for its open-air cafés, inviting *trattorie*, galleries, street vendors and late-night bars.

➕ G4 ✉ 20121 🚌 61; tram 1, 27

MUSEO D'ARTE E SCIENZA

www.museoarteescienza.com.

Near the castle, this fascinating private museum shows you how to tell the difference between genuine and fake antiques—some 2,000 of them.

➕ G4 ✉ Via Q. Sella 4, 20121 ☎ 02 7202 2488 🕐 Mon–Fri 10–6, Sat 10–2 Ⓜ Cairoli, Lanza 🚌 57, 61; tram 1, 4, 7, 27 ♿ None 🖐 Expensive; free for under 10s and over 60s

SAN SIMPLICIANO

This handsome basilica is the finest of the churches in the Brera quarter. It was founded in the fourth century, possibly by Sant'Ambrogio, and reconstructed in the 12th century.

➕ G4 ✉ Piazza San Simpliciano 7, 20121 ☎ 02 862 274 🕐 Mon–Sat 7.10–12, 3–7; Sun 7.30–12.30, 4–7 Ⓜ Lanza 🚌 57, 61; tram 12, 14 ♿ Good 🖐 Free

Down the Via Brera in a Milanese tram

Some Milanese Treasures

This gentle walk takes you from the castle via one of the finest churches in the city to the park and into the bohemian Brera district.

DISTANCE: 3.5km (2.2 miles) **ALLOW:** Half a day with stops

x

Shopping

10 CORSO COMO
www.10corsocomo.com
For sheer style don't miss this fabulous store on the fashionable Corso Como. A stunning array of men's and women's fashions, accessories, homewares, books and CDs and something for the little ones, too. Restaurant, B&B and library on the premises as well.
🔢 G2 ✉ Corso Como 10, 20154 ☎ 02 2900 2674 Ⓜ Garibaldi

BUSCEMI DISCHI
www.buscemi.com
One of the city's oldest and most famous record stores, split between two shops. Don't hesitate to ask for assistance if you can't find what you want on the often crammed shelves.
🔢 F5 ✉ Corso Magenta 31, 20123 ☎ 02 804 103 Ⓜ Cadorna

CARTOLERIA RUFFINI
See the craftsmen at work out the back producing handmade notebooks, albums, boxes and letter racks, which are then sold at the front of this traditional old shop.
🔢 E5 ✉ Via Ruffini 1, 20123 ☎ 02 463 074 Ⓜ Conciliazione

DIEGO DELLA PALMA
Lipsticks, powders and paints from this household name among Italy's make-up elite. Knowledgeable staff can advise you on the products to use to suit your skin tone.
🔢 G4 ✉ Via Madonnina 15, 20121 ☎ 02 876 818 Ⓜ Lanza

FRANCO SABATELLI
www.sabatelli.com
Exclusive picture framer of international repute who sells and restores frames dating from the 16th century.
🔢 G4 ✉ Via Fiori Chiari 5, 20121 ☎ 02 805 2688 Ⓜ Lanza

LA FUNGHERIA
To the west of Corso Magenta you will find quality mushrooms and truffles in this shop, known in Milan for its organic methods. It's worth the little extra journey to get that unusual gift to take home.
🔢 B5 ✉ Via Marghera 14, 20149 ☎ 02 439 0089 Ⓜ Wagner, De Angeli

---

IS IT ANTIQUE?

When searching for that special piece, bear in mind that under Italian law an antique need only be made of old materials. For this reason, what would be called reproduction elsewhere is quite legally called an antique in Italy. Hundreds of shops all over Milan sell so-called antiques, but the narrow, cobbled lanes of the Brera district and the canal area are particularly pleasant places to browse.

MASTRI CARTAI EDITORI
Refined handmade paper in unconventional shades and designs is used to produce innovative items such as lampholders, picture frames and books.
🔢 G4 ✉ Corso Garibaldi 26/34, 20121 ☎ 02 8052 3111 Ⓜ Lanza

MERCATO D'ANTIQUARIATO DI BRERA
Enthusiasts should not miss this monthly antiques market of about 70 stalls laden with collectables at bargain prices.
🔢 G4 ✉ Via Fiori Chiari, 20121 🕐 3rd Sun of month 8.30–6 Ⓜ Lanza

OLD ENGLISH FURNITURE
www.gracis.com
If you like 18th- and 19th-century English furniture, head for this shop, which has many examples on display.
🔢 G4 ✉ Piazza San Simpliciano 6, 20121 ☎ 02 877 807 Ⓜ Lanza

PANTON'S ENGLISH BOOKSHOP
www.englishbookshop.it
The most varied selection of English-language fiction and nonfiction books in Milan; also videos, audio books and a large kids' section.
🔢 D5 ✉ Via Mascheroni 12, 20145 ☎ 02 469 4468 Ⓜ Conciliazione

Entertainment and Nightlife

BAR MAGENTA
www.barmagenta.it
Friendly staff, wooden tables and a top shelf stacked full of the world's finest spirits. Every type of music from jazz to rock and punk is played on the bar's stereo system. Popular with students and fans of sport—particularly Italian football—so it can get noisy.
➕ F5 ✉ Via Carducci 13, 20123 ☎ 02 8053 3808 Ⓜ Cordusio

CRT TEATRO DELL'ARTE
www.teatrocrt.it
Most performances are in Italian but the passionate music and contemporary dance displays will need no translation. Several yearly dance festivals with top directors, dancers and actors.
➕ E4 ✉ Viale Alemagna 6, 20121 ☎ 02 8901 1644 Ⓜ Cadorna

GLORIA
This renovated cinema comprises two theatres, the Garbo and the Marilyn. Big screens and a good sound system. Bar.
➕ D5 ✉ Corso Vercelli 18, 20144 ☎ 02 4800 8908 Ⓜ Pagano, Conciliazione

HOLLYWOOD
www.discotecahollywood.com
Getting in is neither cheap nor easy—you'll need lots of cash and your latest Galleria Emanuele outfit. But once inside you could be rubbing shoulders with Milan's beautiful people.
➕ G2 ✉ Corso Como 15, 20154 ☎ 02 659 8996 Ⓜ Garibaldi

JAMAICA
www.jamaicabar.it
Since 1920, Brera's painters and artists have flocked to this legendary haunt, and it's still popular today. The cocktails and huge salads are good.
➕ G4 ✉ Via Brera 32, 20121 ☎ 02 876 723 Ⓜ Montenapoleone

OLD FASHION CAFÉ
www.oldfashion.it
Exclusive nightspot in a former ballroom that attracts a chic crowd to its theme nights.
➕ E4 ✉ Viale E. Alemagna 6, 20121 ☎ 02 805 6231 Ⓜ Cadorna

TEATRO LITTA
www.teatrolitta.it
Children's plays make up the lion's share of performances in this theatre, in the striking Palazzo Litta. The magic and dance displays will delight English-speaking kids, although the Italian language drama shows may be beyond them. A peek inside the classic baroque theatre is worth it for those interested in architecture.
➕ F5 ✉ Corso Magenta 24, 20123 ☎ 02 8645 4545 Ⓜ Cadorna

TEATRO SMERALDO
www.smeraldo.it
Smeraldo is particularly popular for its musicals such as *Chicago*, which played in 2004, and *Jesus Christ Superstar* in 2003. The theatre seats over 2,000 people and is also a venue for dance, drama and concerts.
➕ G2 ✉ Piazza XXV Aprile 10, 20154 ☎ 02 2900 6767 Ⓜ Moscova, Garibaldi

TOCQUEVILLE
www.tocqueville13.it
Celebrity spotting is top of the bill at the ultracool Thursday and Sunday night parties. Feast on tapas all night.
➕ G2 ✉ Via de Tocqueville 13, 20154 ☎ 02 2900 2973 Ⓜ Garibaldi

---

DANCING TRENDS
Milan is the place to be if you are on the lookout for new music and dance trends. The city boasts hoards of discos and clubs that offer all types of music but the trend tends to lean toward a select few. Apart from the rare exceptions, clubs and discos change their name and style on a regular basis. A club that is in vogue one week can be passé the next. Entrance fees vary a lot—a system known as 'drinkcard', where you pay for your drinks at the door, is often used. Some places are free to get in but you will pay, probably over the top, for drinks.

Restaurants

PRICES

Prices are approximate, based on a 3-course meal for one person.

€€€ over €50
€€   €20–€50
€   under €20

ALL'ISOLA (€–€€)

This is more than an excellent *pizzeria*, the restaurant serves steaks and pasta as well as fresh fish and Mediterranean specialties. The pizzas, however, are the perfect choice, cooked in a wood fire.

✚ G2 ✉ Corso Como 10, 20154 ☎ 02 657 1624 🕐 Thu–Tue lunch, dinner, Wed dinner only 🚇 Garibaldi

BIFFI (€€)

Biffi has been around since the end of the 19th century and is the place to try their own *panettone*. Come here for breakfast before shopping or for an aperitif afterward.

✚ D5 ✉ Corso Magenta 87, 20123 ☎ 02 4800 6702 🕐 Tue–Sun 🚇 Conciliazione

BINDI (€)

For mouthwatering cream cakes and pastries drop in at this bright and cheery local café, close to the castle and park.

✚ F5 ✉ Piazale Cardorna 9, 20123 ☎ 02 8645 1178 🕐 Mon–Sat 🚇 Cadorna

C'ERA UNA VOLTA (€€)

The atmosphere at this *trattoria* changes with the time of day: Lunch is relaxed, loud and crowded with office workers; for dinner it's tablecloths, candles and couples sharing a romantic meal. Good pasta and fish dishes.

✚ G3 ✉ Via Palermo 20, 20121 ☎ 02 654 060 🕐 Mon–Sat lunch, dinner, Sun dinner 🚇 Moscova

IL CONSOLARE (€€)

Airy, bright restaurant that focuses on fish; try the *orata* (sea bream). Popular with locals.

✚ G5 ✉ Via Ciovasso 3, 20121 ☎ 02 805 3581 🕐 Wed–Sat lunch, dinner; Tue dinner only 🚇 Cairoli, Lanza

JUST CAVALLI CAFÉ (€€€)

Designer Roberto Cavalli's hot spot in the Parco Sempione at the base of the Torre Branca. The semicircular steel and glass structure encloses a sophisticated restaurant with African-style accessories. Here you can sip cocktails with celebrities and choose dishes from worldwide cuisines. Garden with a gazebo.

✚ E4 ✉ Viale Luigi Cameons, Torre Branca, 20121 ☎ 02 311 817 🕐 Mon–Sat dinner, Sun lunch only 🚇 Cadorna

ORIENT EXPRESS (€€€)

www.orient-express.it

In one of the most picturesque streets in the Brera district, this restaurant recreates scenes from the Orient Express; first-class dining in the intimate luxury of a railway carriage.

✚ G4 ✉ Via Fiori Chiari 8, 20121 ☎ 02 805 6227 🕐 Mon–Sat lunch, dinner; Sun brunch only 🚇 Lanza

ROCKING HORSE (€€)

At the north end of Corso Como, this is a nice place to eat salads, pizzas and pastas alfresco.

✚ G2 ✉ Corso Como 12 , 20154 ☎ 02 657 0433 🕐 Daily lunch, dinner 🚇 Garibaldi

VIEL (€)

www.viel-milano.it

Viel has been in business producing natural ice cream since the 1940s. This is one of four branches in the city. Delicious selection of fresh fruit.

✚ G4 ✉ Corso Garibaldi 12, 20121 ☎ 02 8691 5489 🕐 Thu–Tue 🚇 Lanza

REGIONAL FISH DISHES

Although Milan does not have a typical Lombardy cuisine, it has embraced the cooking of the surrounding area. The fish market in Milan is one of the finest in Italy, and you will find the freshest fish and seafood on many restaurant menus. A visit to the lakes gives you the chance to sample some good local fish, such as carp or tench, while the restaurants in the areas close to the River Po serve eel and catfish.

Probably not the most attractive part of the city, but this area does feature some of the most striking churches in Milan. And for alternative shopping at lower prices Corso di Porto Ticinese fits the bill.

5

6

7

8

9

VIALE DI PORTA VERCELLINA

Via Bandello

Via San

Via M

Via C

Olivetani

Via B Zenale

Via C De Grassi

Via A De Togni

Via G Mellerio

Via G Marradi

Via Teramati

Via C CARDUCCI

Via Olgiata

Piazza Ambrogio

P

De Meis

Teatro d Marionette

Via Vittore

Piazza S Vittore

S Vittore al Corpo ✕

Basilica di Sant'Ambrogio

P

Museo Nazionale della Scienza e della Tecnologia L da Vinci

S Ambrogio

P

Via Vico

Piazza G Filangieri

P

Via Olona

S Ambrogio ✕

Monast S Michele S Dosse

Pusterla di S Ambrogio

Univ Cattolica

VIA

Via Muma Pompilio

Via P Azario

VIALE

Via Carroccio

Via Lesmi

Via Ausonio

Via S Vincenzo

Piazza S Agostino

S Agostino

Via Modestino

PAPINIANO

Via Cesare da

Via D sesto

Via Crespi

S Vincenzo in Prato

Ariberto

Ariberto d'Oggio

P

CORSO GENOVA

Porta Genova

Via G Codara

Via C Simonett

Via C Ferra

VIALE

Via C

Darsena

0 ————— 250 m
0 ————— 250 yds

D   **E**

Via Nirone
Via S Valeria
argo Via S
A Gemelli
Via L Necchi
Palazzo
Stanga
Via S Pio V
Cappuccio
Via S Orsola
Palazzo
Borromeo
Piazza
Borromeo
Via Corani
Via Borromeo
Piazza
Mentana
Via Circo
Via S Marta
Palazzo
Visconti
Via S Sisto
Via Medici
Via S Nerino
Piazza
S Giorgio
Carrobbio
S Maria Valle
Torino
Via
Lanzone
Largo
d'Carrobbio
Via
Largo
Gallarati
Via S M Valle
Caminadella
San
Bernardino
Correnti
Carrobbio
Stampa
Via C Correnti
Ticinese
Carrobbio
Via
Vito
Ars
Via Fabbri
Via G G Mora
Via di Porta Ticinese
Piazza
d'Vetra
Piazza
S Quasimodo
Piazza
Resist
artigiana
Resistenza
Partigiana
AMICIS
Via Torti
Colonne di
S Lorenzo
San Lorenzo
Maggiore
S M Vittoria
VIA
MOLINO
D ARMI
Conca
del
Naviglio
Anfiteatro
Romano
Molino
delle Armi
Ticinese
Via A Banfi
Via d Chiusa
oggiono
Arena
Via
Parco delle
Basiliche
Croce
Via
Vettabbia
Ronconi
Vetere
Via Scaldasole
Via di
Corso di
Porta Ticinese
Porta
Museo
Diocesano
Santa
Via Calatafimi
ANNUNZIO
Via Pranzeri
S Eustorgio /
24 Maggio
Corso
di
Basilica di
Sant'Eustorgio
Piazza
S Eustorgio
Porta Ticinese
Via
Sambuco
Navigli
Plazza XXIV
Maggio
VIALE G GALEAZZO

F
G

Basilica di Sant'Ambrogio

HIGHLIGHTS

● Sarcophagus of Stilicho
● 10th-century *ciborium* (canopy)
● Ninth-century altar front sculpted by Volvinio and encrusted with gems, gold and silver
● Chapel of San Vittore in Ciel d'Oro, with fifth-century dome mosaic
● Underground crypt with remains of saints Ambrogio, Gervasius and Portasius in a single urn

TIP

● There is an annual market on St. Ambrogio's day, 7th December, with stalls around the church. Expect crowds.

Named for the city's patron saint, Sant'Ambrogio is a supreme example of Romanesque architecture and a prototype for many 11th- and 12th-century Lombard churches.

Years in the building The church, west of the Duomo, was originally built between AD379 and 386 by Bishop Ambrogio, who was later made patron saint of Milan. The church was enlarged in the ninth and 11th centuries, although Bramante's Portico della Canonica was left unfinished until the 17th century, and had to be reconstructed after the 1943 bombings.

Superb decoration This is one of the loveliest churches in the city, occupying a large complex with lots to see. The fine redbrick exterior, with its two

The atrium of the Basilica of Sant'Ambrogio, one of Milan's finest churches (main picture below). Christ the Redeemer with symbols of the evangelists and apostles, a detail of the front of the antependium (below right). Views of the bell tower and details of the architecture (bottom right)

bell towers (ninth-century one to the right, 12th-century one to the left) is best seen from Piazza Sant'Ambrogio. Access to the church is via the lovely Ansperto atrium, which was built as a refuge for pilgrims. The church interior, simple and harmonious, has three aisles and distinctive ribbed cross vaulting. The apse is embellished with mosaics (sixth- to eighth-century, much restored) depicting Christ between Milanese saints and martyrs.

Not to be missed Beautifully carved in the fourth century, the Sarcophagus of Stilicho, below the pulpit and left of the nave, is traditionally believed to be the tomb of the Roman Military Commander Stilicho and his wife and is one of the few surviving features of the original church. The pulpit above it was constructed from 12th-century fragments.

THE BASICS

✚ F6
✉ Piazza Sant'Ambrogio 15, 20123
☎ 02 8645 0895
🕐 Mon–Sat 7–12, 2.30–7; Sun, holidays 7–1, 3–8. No visits during services
🚇 Sant'Ambrogio
🚌 50, 58, 94
♿ Good; entrance on Via Lanzone 30
🎟 Free; Chapel of San Vittore in Ciel d'Oro inexpensive

Museo Nazionale della Scienza e della Tecnologia

HIGHLIGHTS

- The Leonardo Gallery
- Leonardo self-portrait
- Watchmaker's workshop (1750)
- Early steam locomotives
- *The Ebe*, a huge schooner
- *The Conte Biancammo*, a 1925 transatlantic liner with period furnishings
- Early computers

TIP

- Choose a wet or dull day to visit as there is plenty to see and do to fill a morning or afternoon.

The Museo Nazionale della Scienza e della Tecnologia 'Leonardo da Vinci' is one of the world's largest science and technology museums, with around 10,000 scientific exhibits and displays.

Early beginnings The oldest of the three museum buildings (the Monumental Building) is the Olivetan Monastery, built in Renaissance style in the 16th century. Although much has been altered, it still has two beautiful cloisters. The site became a military hospital and barracks under Napoleon. It opened as a museum in 1953 with an exhibition on Leonardo da Vinci, to coincide with the fifth centenary of his birth.

Vast collections Within the labyrinthine museum are 16 interactive laboratories where visitors can

The cloisters of the early 16th-century Olivetan Monastery—home to the Science Museum (far left). The schooner Ebe in the Naval Pavilion (left). Blowing bubbles in an interactive workshop (right). Hands-on ceramics (bottom left). Galleria Leonardo da Vinci (bottom middle). Steam locomotives in the Railway Pavilion (bottom right)

learn all about science and technology, engaging in cutting-edge issues such as robotics and bio-technologies; children especially enjoy the hands-on approach. There are also two separate buildings, devoted to rail, air and sea transport. Steam and electric trains are in the reconstructed art nouveau station (the Train Pavilion), and aircraft and ships can be found in the Aero-Maritime Pavilion.

Planning your visit This museum can appear vast and daunting the first time you visit so decide what you most want to see before your visit. The Leonardo Gallery is fascinating, though most of the explanations are in Italian only. If you take children, it's best to head for the interactive labs, huge boats, steam trains, and aircraft. You can also visit the submarine *Toti* outside the Monumental Building.

THE BASICS

www.museoscienza.org

➕ E6

✉ Via San Vittore 21, 20123

☎ 02 485 551

🕐 Tue–Fri 9.30–5, Sat, Sun, public holidays 9.30–6.30

🍴 Refreshment area

Ⓜ Sant'Ambrogio

🚌 50, 58, 94

♿ Good

💲 Expensive

❓ Guided tours every Sat afternoon and Sun (full day). It is possible to organize guided tours in English

San Lorenzo Maggiore

A replica of the Roman statue of Constantine (left) and a good meeting place (below)

THE BASICS

✚ F7

✉ Corso di Porta Ticinese 39, 20123

☎ 02 8940 4129

🕐 Daily 7.30–6.45; Capella di Sant'Aquilino daily 9.30–6.30

Ⓜ Missori

🚌 94; tram 3

♿ Good

✎ Free; Capella di Sant'Aquilino inexpensive

HIGHLIGHTS

● Capella di Sant'Aquilino
● Fourth/fifth-century mosaics
● 12th-century fresco
● The view of the church from Parco delle Basiliche, the garden behind the church

This huge fourth-century basilica may have been the chapel of the imperial Roman palace. The greatest treasure is the Sant'Aquilino Chapel, once entirely covered in frescoes and mosaics.

Founded on a Roman temple The church can be found in the Ticinese quarter, outside the Roman walls, southwest of the city. It is also known as San Lorenzo alle Colonne, named after the colonnade outside the church, dating from the second and third centuries. The 16 columns and the section of architrave were probably part of a temple and were placed here in the fourth century when construction began on the basilica. Built with marble from Roman buildings nearby, the basilica was founded on what was thought to be a Roman amphitheatre. It was subsequently rebuilt in the 12th century, with further rebuilding between 1573 and 1619 by Martino Bassi.

Beautiful chapel You can't miss the church—it has the largest dome in Milan. The interior, octagonal in form and crowned by the dome, is striking for its sheer size. Inside, make for the Capella di Sant'Aquilino, which may have been added as a mausoleum; its small chapel houses the saint's remains in a silver urn. The 12th-century fresco *The Deposition* can be seen at the entrance to the chapel, on the left-hand side. Here you will find the remarkable fourth- or fifth-century mosaics of *Christ and the Apostles*, and *Elijah on the Chariot of Fire*. Steps behind the altar take you down to the foundations of the church.

More to See

BASILICA DI SANT'EUSTORGIO

The unassuming neo-Romanesque façade of the Basilica of Sant'Eustorgio belies the wonderful earlier interior architecture and superb frescoes, which make this one of the most interesting churches to visit in the city. The original church was founded by St. Eustorgius in the fourth century but was completely destroyed by Frederick Barbarossa in 1162. Reconstruction began in 1190 and lasted for several centuries. This included the building of the bell tower in 1306, the first in Milan to be fitted with a clock. The final alteration came in 1865 with the building of the façade seen today. The monastery adjoining the church is the property of the Diocesan museum and has 17th- and 18th-century religious relics and art from the Basilica.
➕ F8 ✉ Piazza Sant'Eustorgio 1, 20122 ☎ Church: 02 8940 2671; museum: 02 5810 1583 🕐 Church: Mon–Sat 7.30–12.30, 3.30–6.30, Sun 7.30–1.15, 3.30–6.30; museum: Tue–Sun 10–6 🚊 Tram 3, 9, 30 ♿ Good (ramp to church) 🎫 Church free; museum moderate

CORSO DI PORTA TICINESE

This street is bisected by one of the remaining medieval gates surrounding the heart of Milan: Porta Ticinese. This area is popular with younger shoppers as its trendy, retro clothing and accessory boutiques are less expensive than the designer shops farther north. Its bohemian atmosphere makes it a fun place to visit and it also has several good traditional *trattorie*.
➕ F7–F8 ✉ Extends from Lago Carrobbio down to Piazza Eustorgio 🚊 Tram 3

PARCO DELLE BASILICHE

Named after the basilicas of San Lorenzo and Sant'Eustorgio, this is a pleasant park in the southeast of the city. A pathway flanked by roses links the two basilicas—with the busy Via Molino delle Armi in between. Once one of the least desirable spots in the city, where public hangings took place and tanners' workshops created a foul stench, it now fortunately affords a more pleasurable experience.
➕ F7 ✉ Southeast of city, 20123 🕐 Dawn–dusk 🚊 94; tram 3

Porta Ticinese—one of the original gateways to the city, leading to Corso di Porta Ticinese, a hot spot for shopping

Museums to Canals

Begin at one of the city's finest museums, visit churches along the way, retreat to peaceful gardens and finish up by the canals.

DISTANCE: 3.2km (2 miles) **ALLOW:** 2 hours plus stops

START

MUSEO NAZIONALE DELLA SCIENZA
🗺 E6 Ⓜ Sant'Ambrogio

END

NAVIGLI
🗺 E8 Ⓜ Porta Genova 🚌 59; tram 2, 3

1 If you are keen on science, visit the Museo Nazionale della Scienza (▷ 84–85) in Via San Vittore. Turn right out of the museum and continue along to cross over Via Carducci.

8 Turning to the right from the piazza brings you to the Navigli (▷ 96) district, an ideal spot to explore or lunch by the canals.

2 Ahead is the lovely Basilica di Sant'Ambrogio (▷ 82–83). Take the path to the left and follow it right the way round the church. Turn right into Piazza Sant'Ambrogio.

7 In the park is the Museo Diocesano, with its fine collection of religious art. At the far end of the park is Sant'Eustorgio (▷ 88). Exit here and turn right alongside the church and then left back onto Corso Ticinese. Carry on down to Piazzale XXIV Maggio.

3 Ahead is the former monastery, now housing the Catholic university. Leave these buildings on your right and take Via Necchi, the next right.

6 Continue to San Lorenzo Maggiore (▷ 86) on your left, and on through the Antica Porta Ticinese, the original entry point into the city. Take the first left for a break in the small park (Basiliche ▷ 88).

4 Carry on into Via San Pio V and then turn left into Via Lazone. At Via Circo look to the left for the remains of the Circo Romano. Back on Lanzone, bear right into Via Torchio.

5 Cross Lago Carrobbio; take the second right into Corso di Porta Ticinese.

THE SOUTHWEST

WALK

Shopping

ANNA FABIANO

It's nice to find a shop where the clothes are cutting edge but are also wearable in everyday situations. No two pieces are exactly the same and they will get you noticed.
🞧 F7 ✉ Corso di Porta Ticinese 40, 20123 ☎ 02 5811 2348 🅜 Missori 🚋 Tram 2, 3

B-FLY

This customized Levi's shop is a real boon for jeans aficionados. All items have been abused enough with scissors, spray cans and threads to be called one-off. The hand-crafting is reflected in the price.
🞧 F7 ✉ Corso di Porta Ticinese 46, 20123 ☎ 02 8942 3178 🅜 Missori 🚋 Tram 2, 3

BIFFI

www.biffi.com
The place to shop for classic men's and women's designer names; watch for new emerging talent. Clothes for the younger customer are across the street.
🞧 F7 ✉ Corso Genova 6, 20123 ☎ 02 831 1601 🅜 Porta Genova

CRAZY FROG

www.crazyfrog.it
Eccentric, original high-quality products, all made in Italy. Everything from bags, belts and accessories to shoes, boots and jewellery has the logo of the little frog. Expensive but definitely classy.

🞧 F7 ✉ Corso di Porta Ticinese 50, 20123 ☎ 02 832 3693 🅜 Missori 🚋 Tram 2, 3

DIESEL

www.diesel.com
Jeans fans should not miss this Diesel Experimental range flagship concept store, where all items are customized.
🞧 F7 ✉ Corso di Porta Ticinese 44, 20123 ☎ 02 8942 0916 🅜 Missori 🚋 Tram 2, 3

MARKETS

Milan's street markets are noisy and fun, selling anything from cheeses and salamis to clothes and second-hand books, plus there are good specialist markets as well. Markets fill the waterfronts around the canals, notably Mercato del Sabato on Viale Papiniano (🞧 E7) on Saturdays, which offers great designer-label bargains in clothes, shoes and bags, and there is a flea market (Fiera di Senigallia) at Darsena, on Viale d'Annunzio (🞧 F8) also on Saturday. A huge antique market stretches alongside the canals on the last Sunday of each month. Elsewhere in the city other good general markets are at Via San Marco (🞧 G3) on Thursday morning, Via Zuretti (🞧 Off map at K1) on Wednesday morning and Via Crema (🞧 K9) on Friday morning.

GIORGIO FEDON 1919

www.giorgiofedon1919.it
Smart, elegant and with cleanest of lines, the leather goods at this old-established store are second to none and with prices to match. Optical accessories and writing implements, too.
🞧 F6 ✉ Lago Carrobbio, 20123 ☎ 02 8691 7500 🅜 Missori 🚋 Tram 2, 3

KALOS

www.kalos-snc.it
Big bold costume jewellery at reasonable prices attractively displayed in a store in the popular shopping street, Porta Ticinese. Rings, bracelets, earrings, necklaces.
🞧 F7 ✉ Corso di Porta Ticinese 50, 20123 ☎ 02 8940 4329 🅜 Missori 🚋 Tram 2, 3

LAZZARI

For up-to-the-minute storage solutions in brightly hued nylon you can't beat Lazzari, with a container for every item in the house.
🞧 F7 ✉ Corso di Porta Ticinese 70, 20123 ☎ 02 837 5163 🅜 Missori 🚋 Tram 2, 3

TESSUTI

Mimma Gini, formerly a furniture designer, has turned to fabrics and clothing. Wonderful use of silks, brocades, velvets and cottons in vivid colours plus great accessories and fabrics to buy.
🞧 G7 ✉ Via Santa Croce 21 20122 ☎ 02 8940 0722 🅜 Missori 🚋 Tram 2, 3

Entertainment and Nightlife

CINEMA GNOMO
Located not far from the university and often frequented by students, this cinema is aimed at aficionados of film. Not your mainstream but some interesting showings including international festival screenings of world cinema.
F6 Via Lanzone 30/a, 20123 02 804 125 Sant'Ambrogio

LE BICICLETTE
www.lebiciclette.com
Sleek, modern bar and restaurant with changing art exhibitions in an area increasingly popular for nightlife. Happy hour and buffet from 6 until 9.30.
F7 Via Torti 4, 20123 02 5810 4325 Sant'Ambrogio

MAMA CAFÉ RESTAURANT
www.mamacafe.it
A good restaurant in the day, the wines and cocktails are the order of the night. On Friday and Saturday nights there is live music.
F7 Via Caminadella 7, 20123 02 8699 5682 Sant'Agostino

OLD FOX PUB
www.oldfoxpub.it.it
Keeping the original fittings of the former local milk bar, this is the quintessential English pub now popular in the city. Good selection of beers and the owners have a penchant for whiskies.

Lots of English pub 'grub', Italian sports on screen and accompanying music. Occasional themed music nights (check first for details). Buffet and happy hour are very good value from 6 until 9.
E7 Piazza Sant'Agostino, 20123 02 8940 2662 Sant'Agostino

PISCINA SOLARI
www.milanosport.it
Take a dip in this glass-covered five-lane pool, overlooking Parco Solari.
D7 Via Montevideo 11, 20144 02 4695 278 Times vary, so phone first Sant'Agostino

---

MILANESE BARS

From the chic and trendy to the more traditional, Milanese bars are sprinkled throughout the city, and most are open all day until 2 or 3am. They serve a vast selection of beers, wines, aperitifs, cocktails and non-alcoholic drinks, and most have a selection of snacks—some double as cafés. Many of Milan's bars have introduced an early-evening 'happy hour' when drinks are cheaper. If you sit down for waiter service you will pay a premium, whether inside or out. The procedure when standing up is to pay for what you want at the cash desk, then take your receipt to the bar and repeat your order.

SCIMMIE
www.scimmie.it
A fantastic, happening venue for jazz, rock, blues, country, folk, flamenco and Brazilian beats. You even get international stars appearing here. Feast on great-value pizza and snacks as you watch the shows. Be early to get a table.
F9 Via Ascanio Sforza 49, 20136 02 8940 2874 Porta Genova

SHU
www.shucafe.it
Cool retro restaurant, music/disco bar. Sophisticated interiors and fusion cuisine make this a trendy venue for cocktails and dinner. The bar champions the work of young artists. Tuesday is art events' night; Thursday disco dancing; Friday Mia Divina+Shu, from aperitifs to disco.
G7 Via Molino delle Armi, 20122 02 5831 5720 Missori

TEATRO ARSENALE
www.teatroarsenale.org
The place to come for searing comedy, cutting-edge dramas and ground-breaking acting by up-and-coming thespians. Tickets are available from the venue itself, near Via Torino, daily from 1pm. Most performances are in Italian only.
F7 Via Correnti 11, 20122 02 8321 1999, information 02 837 5896 Sant'Ambrogio

Restaurants

PRICES

Prices are approximate, based on a 3-course meal for one person.

€€€   over €50
€€   €20–€50
€   under €20

BE BOP (€)

Pizza with nice thin, crispy bases. For those wanting something else there's also a selection of pasta, salads and snacks. Cooking is also directed at vegetarians and coeliacs, with 90 per cent of the menu gluten free. Pleasant gardens.
➕ G8 ✉ Viale Col di Lana 4, 20136 ☎ 02 837 6972 🕐 All day 🚇 Porta Genova 🚋 Tram 3

CANTINA DELLA VETRA (€€)

One of the few top-drawer real Italian restaurants, close to the Porta Ticinese and the San Lorenzo ruins. Giant slabs of lasagne, stew, hearty pastas and grilled meats.
➕ G7 ✉ Piazza Vetra 5, 20123 ☎ 02 894 0384 🕐 Mon–Sat lunch, dinner; Sun dinner only 🚇 Missori 🚋 Tram 2, 3

CIRIBOGA (€–€€)

A taste of the Mediterranean in both cuisine and sunny décor in a relaxed ambience. Seasonal produce used.
➕ E7 ✉ Via Savona 10, 21044 ☎ 02 832 2496 🕐 Tue–Sun lunch, dinner, Mon dinner only 🚇 Sant'Agostino

GELATERIA LE COLONNE (€)

Good selection of home-made ice creams. Also serves crepes.
➕ F7 ✉ Corso di Porta Ticinese 75, 20123 ☎ 02 837 2292 🕐 Daily 🚇 Missori 🚋 Tram 2, 3

IL GIARDINETTO (€€)

www.osteriailgiardinetto.it Attractive, warm *osteria* resplendent with plants. Excellent cuisine based on Milanese and Placentian tradition.
➕ E8 ✉ Via Tortona 19, 21044 ☎ 02 839 3807 🕐 Mon–Fri lunch, dinner, Sat dinner 🚇 Sant'Agostino

OSTERIA DEI BINARI (€€)

In summer you can eat outside in one of the nicest gardens in Milan.

TRATTORIA OR *OSTERIA*?

In general, a trattoria is an unpretentious, family-run concern, often with a regular clientele of local people who drop in when they do not want to cook for themselves. The *osteria* used to be the most basic of all, where simple dishes were washed down with jugs of local wine. But beware: recently the name has been adopted by some of the most expensive or touristy establishments. You can usually follow the guidelines that the smarter the premises, the more expensive the restaurant.

Specializes in dishes from Lombardy and Piedmont. Friendly service.
➕ E8 ✉ Via Tortona 1, 20144 ☎ 02 8940 6753 🕐 Mon–Sat dinner only 🚇 Porta Genova

RISTORANTE SANT' EUSTORGIO (€€)

Nice venue overlooking the square and the church, just off Porta Ticinese. Stop here for a pizza or traditional dish. Good homemade food from fresh local produce.
➕ F8 ✉ Piazza Sant'Eustorgio 6, 20122 ☎ 02 5810 1396 🕐 Tue–Sun lunch, dinner, Mon dinner only 🚇 Missori 🚋 Tram 2, 3

SUDD (€€)

On a side road off Corso Porta Ticinese leading to the park, elegant Sudd opened in September 2006. Under the same ownership as the Ristorante Sant'Eustorgio (▷ above), it prides itself on traditional cooking, particularly of the southern region of Italy. Piano bar.
➕ F7 ✉ Via Vetere 9, 20122 ☎ 02 5810 8106 🕐 Mon–Fri lunch, dinner, Sat, Sun dinner only 🚇 Missori 🚋 Tram 2, 3

TRATTORIA ALL'ANTICA (€–€€)

Memorable Milanese and Lombard cuisine. Small and very popular, so reserve in advance.
➕ D7 ✉ Via Montevideo 4, 20144 ☎ 02 5810 4360 🕐 Mon–Fri lunch, dinner, Sat dinner only 🚇 Sant'Agostino

There's lots to see and do outside the restraints of the city; stroll the Navigli (canal) district, take in a game of football at the San Siro stadium, or in less than an hour you can be beside magical Lake Como.

Navigli

Now being spruced up, the Navigli area is central to eating out and nightlife in the city

THE BASICS

➕ E8–B9
✉ Extends west of Piazza Maggio along Ripa di Porta Ticinese and south along Alzaia Naviglio Pavese
🚇 Porta Genova
🚌 59; tram 2, 3
♿ Accessible; some steps over bridges

HIGHLIGHTS

● Excellent selection of restaurants and bars
● Antiques market on last Sunday of each month
● Boat trips

Named after the navigable canals, this quarter of the city was once an important trade route for barges. Since barge transport ceased in 1979, the Navigli has gradually evolved into a popular arty and nightlife area.

Decades of neglect Don't expect pristine, picture-postcard canals; the area is still in the early days of extensive renovation. Until recently most money was invested in other parts of the city, the canals considered nothing but an eyesore. But the potential has at long last been recognized. The murky waters are still being dredged of debris, the towpaths rebuilt and the paving stones renewed. In winter the canals can be a disappointment, when they are drained and cleaned up ready for the summer, when it is possible to take a pleasurable two-hour boat tour.

Hive of industry The Navigli was once a working-class area with small artisan workshops lining the towpaths. With the increasing 'gentrification' of the district and the rising costs of rents, these workshops have been pushed out to make way for shops, bars and restaurants—from old family-type *osterias* to sleek, trendy establishments.

After dark As the district develops, the back streets leading off from the canals are filling up with cocktail bars and disco-pubs, attracting a younger clientele. With continuing investment in the area, it is anticipated the Navigli will become the hippest place in town.

Santa Maria della Passione

Mellow bathed in sunlight, Santa Maria della Passione (right) has some fine detail (left)

The second-largest church in Milan after the Duomo, it is distinctive for its handsome dome. But the main attraction is the art within the church—a gallery of 16th- and 17th-century paintings and frescoes by leading Lombard artists.

Elaborate additions Santa Maria della Passione was built in the late 14th to early 15th centuries in a Greek Cross plan and was extended with a nave and side chapels in 1573. The baroque façade, decorated with statues, was added in 1729 by Giuseppe Rusnati, who also built the adjoining convent, now the Conservatorio di Musica Giuseppe Verdi.

Artistic masterpieces The paintings and frescoes that decorate most of the church depict the Passion of Christ or similar themes. The paintings of saints perched on the piers of the nave are by Daniele Crespi. The church has numerous paintings by this Milanese master, considered the finest Lombard painter of the early 17th century. He died in his early 30s of the plague, but his output was considerable. In the first chapel on the left is Crespi's *Il Digiuno di San Carlo* (*The Fasting of St. Charles*), which shows San Carlo Borromeo, Archbishop of Milan and mastermind of the Counter-Reformation. This is Crespi's best-known work and is generally regarded as the most famous 17th-century Milanese painting. It shows the saint with a loaf of bread and a carafe of water—a simple, austere composition reflecting the spirit of the Counter-Reformation.

THE BASICS

🔲 J6
✉ Via Conservatorio 14, 20122
☎ 02 7602 1370
🕐 Mon–Sat 7–12, 3.30–6, Sun and public holidays 7–12, 3.30–6.15
Ⓜ San Babila
🚌 54, 61
♿ Good; one step
💰 Free
ℹ If you have time, peek into the Giuseppe Verdi Conservatory of Music next door to the church to see the striking courtyard

HIGHLIGHTS

● Works by Daniele Crespi
● *The Last Supper* (1543), Gaudenzio Ferrari
● *Deposition* (1510), Bernardino Luini
● The church organs on either side of the choir, with beautiful 16th- and 17th-century carvings and shutters painted by Daniele Crespi

More to See

AQUATICA
www.parcoaquatica.com

A great family day out in the suburbs at San Siro, this water park has pools, thrilling slides, fountains, tubes, river rides and artificial beaches for relaxing.
➕ Off map at A5 ✉ Via G Airaghi 61, 20153 ☎ 02 4820 0134 🕐 Jun–Aug daily 10–7, 🚇 De Angeli then bus 72, Primaticcio then bus 64, Lotto then bus 423 💶 Expensive

CIMITERO MONUMENTALE

The neo-Romanesque cemetery (1866) covers an area of 250,000sq m (900,000sq ft) in the northwest of the city. Eminent Milanese and other Italians, including novelist Manzoni and the poet Salvatore Quasimodo, are buried in the Famae Aedes (House of Fame). Fine sculpture.
➕ F1 ✉ Piazzale Cimitero Monumentale, north end of Via Manzoni, 20154 ☎ 02 8846 5600 🕐 Tue–Sat 8–6 🚋 43, 70 tram 3, 4, 7, 11, 12, 14, 29, 30, 33 ♿ Good 💶 Free

GIARDINO DELLA GUASTALLA

The oldest public gardens in Milan, founded in 1555 by Paola Ludovica Torelli, Countess of Guastalla, who planned it as part of the Guastalla College for daughters of impoverished local nobles. There are several monuments and a fish pond.
➕ J7 ✉ Via San Barnaba, 20122 🕐 Daily 8–4 (longer hours in summer) 🚋 60, 77; tram 12, 27

LEONARDO'S HORSE

The largest bronze equine statue in the world at 7m (24ft) high, this is a replica of a monument that Leonardo da Vinci was commissioned to build in 1482. However, it didn't get beyond model stage, and was finally cast in 1999 in the US. It rather appropriately stands outside the horse-racing stadium, the Ippodrome (▷ 103) in San Siro.
➕ Off map at A2 ✉ Piazzale dello Sport, San Siro 20151 🚇 Lotto 🚋 Tram 16

MUSEO DEL GIOCATTOLO E DEL BAMBINO
www.museodelgiocattolo.it

A huge toy museum about 3km (2 miles) east of the city. Displays include 18th-century handcrafted toys,

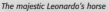

The majestic Leonardo's horse

tin science-fiction toys and papier-maché dolls from the 1950s and 1960s. Exhibits take on various themes, such as Pinocchio, the Golden Age of the Toy (1880–1915), the theatre and circus.
🔢 Off map at A5 ✉ Via Pitteri 56, 20134 ☎ 02 2641 1585 🕐 Mon–Fri 9.30–4, Sat, Sun, holidays 9.30–12.30, 3–6 🚇 Lambrate, then bus 75 ♿ Good 💲 Moderate

MUSEO INTER & AC MILAN
This museum, Italy's first museum dedicated entirely to sport, is in the San Siro stadium, where both of Milan's soccer teams play. There are more than 3,000 items on display, including trophies, flags, soccer shirts, boots and other memorabilia relating to Milan's two famous teams, Inter and AC. There are guided tours of the stadium every day except Sunday and when matches are in progress.
🔢 Off map at A2 ✉ Stadio Giuseppe Meazza (San Siro), Gate 21, Via Piccolomini 5, 20151 ☎ 02 404 2432 🕐 Daily 10–6 (last entry 5); the museum is closed during sporting events 🚇 Lotto, then shuttle bus for matches; tram 16 ♿ Good 💲 Expensive

PARCO LAMBRO
This large park (over 90ha/222 acres) to the east of the city is a good place to relax and escape the heat and noise of Milan in high summer. It was designed to mirror the natural Lombardy countryside with the River Lambro meandering through the middle and has numerous small lakes and ponds. Team sports and rowing are popular activities here.
🔢 Off map at M1 🚇 Udine 🚌 55

STAZIONE CENTRALE
Stazione Centrale is not just Milan's main railway station. It is the biggest in Italy and is a majestic building that commands great respect architecturally. Although it was not completed until 1931, it was designed in 1912 and its style is more characteristic of the art nouveau movement than the heavy Fascist architecture of the 1930s.
🔢 K1 ✉ Piazzale Duca d'Aosta, 20124 ☎ 02 7252 4360 🕐 24 hours, tourist information Mon–Sat 8–7, Sun 9–12.30, 1.30–6 🚇 Centrale 🚌 42, 60, 82, 92; tram 2, 5, 33 💲 Good

Get away from it all in the attractive Parco Lambro

Excursions

THE BASICS

Distance 48km (30 miles)
Journey time 1 hour
🚆 Regular service from Garibaldi FS
ℹ️ Via Gombito 13
☎ 035 242 226;
www.apt.bergamo.it

BERGAMO

Northeast of Milan in the southern foothills of the Alps, Bergamo could not be more different from Italy's business capital.

Remarkably unspoiled, historic Bergamo crowns a steep hill. The city is divided into the medieval Città Alta (Upper Town), within 16th-century walls, and the contrasting modern, traffic-filled Città Bassa (Lower Town). A funicular transports you to Città Alta and its picturesque cobbled alleyways and medieval and Renaissance buildings. Visit Piazza del Duomo, where the Duomo pales against the Renaissance porch of the Basilica of Santa Maria Maggiore and lavish façade of the Cappella Colleoni. The highlight of the lower town is the Galleria Accademia Carrara and its collection of Venetian, Bergamesque and other works of art.

THE BASICS

Distance 93km (58 miles)
Journey time 2 hours
🚆 Regular service from Stazione Centrale
ℹ️ Piazza del Comune 5
☎ 0372 23233;
www.aptcremona.it

CREMONA

A quiet market town on the banks of the River Po, Cremona has been the heart of the violin-making industry since 1566.

The greatest violin maker, Antonio Stradivari, was born here in 1644, and is commemorated in the Museo Stradivariano, where many of his tools are on display. In the middle of town is Piazza del Comune, a fine medieval square with beautiful medieval monuments: the highest bell tower in Italy, the Romanesque/Gothic cathedral, the octagonal Baptistery (1167) and the Palazzo del Comune (1206–45). The Palazzo del Comune has a collection of historic violins, including examples by Amati and Stradivari.

LAKE COMO

Its temperate climate and lavish villas make Como the most romantic of the three major Italian lakes. Enjoy boating trips, walks in the mountains, visits to lakeshore villas and wonderful views.

Surrounded by high mountains and rugged hills, Lake Como has inspired writers, artists and musicians from Pliny the Younger in Roman times to 19th-century Romantics such as French novelists Stendhal and Flaubert. Today it also draws celebrities. The first steamboat was launched from here in 1826 and visitors have been taking boat trips to enjoy the views of lakeside ever since. Como is smaller than Lake Maggiore and Garda but it has the longest perimeter (over 170km/106 miles) and at its deepest point, between Argegno and Nesso, it measures 410m (1,345ft), making it the deepest lake in Italy.

THE BASICS

Distance 50km (31 miles)
Journey time 30 minutues/1 hour depending on departure station
🚆 Regular service from Stazione Centrale to Como town (30 minutes); Cardorna (1 hour)
ℹ️ Piazza Cavour 17, 22100 Como ☎ 031 3300111; www.lakecomo.com

PAVIA

Pavia is graced by fine Romanesque and medieval buildings, but what really draws the crowds is the nearby 14th-century monastery.

Certosa di Pavia (8km/5 miles north of Pavia) is one of the most extravagant religious complexes in Northern Italy—the exuberant façade in multi-toned marble has a wealth of inlay and sculpture. Inside there is a profusion of Renaissance and baroque art. Pavia's rich heritage of art and architecture is reflected in its Renaissance cathedral, whose architects include Leonardo da Vinci, Bramante and Amadeo, several fine medieval churches and the Visconti castle.

THE BASICS

Distance 39km (24 miles)
Journey time 45 minutes
🚆 Service from Stazione Centrale to Famagosta station, then 15-minute walk
ℹ️ Via Fabio Filzi 2 ☎ 0382 22156; www.apt.pv.it

FARTHER AFIELD

EXCURSIONS

AC MILAN AND INTER

www.acmilan.com or www.inter.it
Catch one of Italy's most illustrious soccer clubs, AC Milan or Inter, at the San Siro stadium on alternate weekends during the season. Tickets for matches sell out fast, so buy in advance from the clubs' shop in Via Turati, from FNAC in Via Torino, on the website or through TicketOne.
➕ Off map at A2 ✉ Via Piccolomini 5, 20151 ☎ 02 4009 2175 🕐 Sep–Jun 🚇 Lotto then free bus before matches 🚋 Tram 16

ALCATRAZ

www.alcatrazmilano.com
Rock-orientated live music and disco venue frequented by the occasional famous face.
➕ Off map at G1 ✉ Via Valtellina 25, 20121 ☎ 02 6901 6352 🚇 Garibaldi

AUDITORIUM DI MILANO

www.auditoriumdimilano.org
A multipurpose hall and the home of the Orchestra Sinfonica di Milano Guiseppe Verdi. Symphony concerts, choral works and chamber music; also jazz and light music.
➕ Off map at F9 ✉ Largo G Mahler, 20136 ☎ 02 8338 9201/2/3 🚇 Romolo, then trolley bus 90, 91 🚋 59, 71

BLUE NOTE

www.bluenotemilano.com
Perfect venue for listening to top-quality international jazz. Also a restaurant and a bar. You get the chance to catch some big international names.
➕ Off map at G1 ✉ Via Borsieri 37, 20159 ☎ 02 690 1688 🚇 Garibaldi

CENTRO SPORTIVO MARIO SAINI

This tennis facility has an open-air clay court and 12 indoor synthetic courts. Equipment is available to rent. Non-members welcome, but tennis whites are appreciated.
➕ Off map at M4 ✉ Via Corelli 136, 20134 ☎ 02 756 1280 🕐 Daily dawn–dusk 🚋 38

MEZZA STADIUM

Renamed after Giuseppe Mezza, one of Italy's all-time great soccer players, in 1980, this famous stadium is more commonly called San Siro, after the district surrounding it. A remarkable design: the building gives the impression that it is wrapped up by the spiralling access flights. It was originally built in 1926 as a gift from Piero Pirelli, the then president of AC Milan, and could only seat 10,000. A second tier was added in 1955 and a third plus a fibre glass roof supported by 12 cylindrical concrete towers was added in 1987, making the stadium's capacity over 85,000. The 1990 World Cup was staged at San Siro.

COLOSSEO

There is a choice of three screens, called the Visconti, Allen and Chaplin—all names with movie connections—plus a bar.
➕ B8 ✉ Viale Monte Nero 84, 20135 ☎ 02 5990 1361 🚇 Porta Romano

DUCALE

www.cinenauta.it/ducale
The Ducale has been converted from an old cinema into a modern four-screen movie house with a pleasant bar.
➕ B8 ✉ Piazza Napoli 27, 20146 ☎ 02 4771 9279 🚇 Porta Genova

GOLF CLUB MILANO

www.golfclubmilano.it
This prestigious 18-hole golf course 30 minutes from Milan is close to the town of Monza. Pro shop, driving range, pool and restaurant.
➕ Off map to north ✉ Viale Mulini San Giorgio 7, 20052 Monza ☎ 039 303 081

IPPODROME DEL GALOPPO/TROTTING

www.trenno.it
For horseracing fans there is a full calendar of flat racing events from March to November. In the separate arena across the road, trotting races take place throughout the year, except for the month of August.
➕ Off map at A2 ✉ Piazzale dello Sport, San Siro 20151 ☎ 02 482 161 🚇 Lotto 🚋 Tram 16

LE ROVEDINE

www.rovedine.com
Milan's only public golf course lies 6km (4 miles) outside the city. Restaurant.
🔢 Off map to east ✉ Via Karl Marx 18, Noverasco di Opera, 20090 ☎ 02 5760 6420

MAGAZZINI GENERALI

A mixed crowd work up a sweat to a good range of music at this nightclub, spread over two floors.
🔢 Off map at J9 ✉ Via Pietrasanta 14, 20141 ☎ 02 5521 1313 🚇 Lodi Tibb

PLASTIC

www.thisisplastic.com
With four bars and three music rooms, this club that has been dancing for 25 years is one of the best in Milan.
🔢 M7 ✉ Viale Umbria 120, 20131 ☎ 02 733 996 🚌 92; Tram 12

PLINIUS

www.multisalaplinius.com
Six screens showing the latest mainstream films.
🔢 M2 ✉ Viale Abruzzi 28–30, 20131 ☎ 02 2953 1103 🚇 Loreto, Lima

POGUE MAHONE

Those who require a night away from the typical Italian bar—to drink Guinness and watch soccer—should head for this popular Irish pub. Occasional live bands.
🔢 K8 ✉ Via Salmini 3, 20135 ☎ 02 5830 9726 🚇 Porta Romana

ROLLING STONE

www.rollingstone.it
Listen to live rock, punk, indie and jazz at this relaxed hangout. No dress code.
🔢 L6 ✉ Corso XXII Marzo 32, 20135 ☎ 02 733172 🚇 Porta Vittorio

TEATRO CARCANO

www.teatrocarcano.com
First opened to the public in 1803, the theatre underwent substantial changes in the 1980s. Theatrical productions include staged versions of films, and it is also used for lectures by the university.
🔢 J7 ✉ Corso di Porta Romana 63, 20122 ☎ 02 5518 1362/5518 1377 🚇 Crocetta

TEATRO CIAK

www.teatrociak.com
A popular venue for a variety of performance styles, including comedy, cabaret and murder mystery plays. A great place to spot emerging talent. Reserve in advance.
🔢 Off map at M4 ✉ Via Sangallo 33, 20133 ☎ 02 7611 0093 🚇 Dateo 🚊 Tram 5

TRANSILVANIA

www.transilvanialive.it
There is more of a youthful feel than most rock clubs at this extremely noisy venue, a hot spot for visiting rockers. Details of live bands are on the website.
🔢 Off map at A4 ✉ Via Paravia 59, 20148 ☎ 02 4871 2578; 🚇 Bande Nere, then bus 95

TROPICANA CLUB LATINO

www.tropicanaclublatino.it
The place to go for Latin-American dancing. A mostly over-thirties crowd move to the rhythm of salsa and tango on three floors.
🔢 H8 ✉ Viale Bligny 52, 20136 ☎ 02 5843 6525 🚇 Porta Romana

TUNNEL

An unusual and unique space created in a converted warehouse under the central station. A variety of live music, DJ evenings, poetry readings, film shows and exhibitions, and you can enjoy cocktails at the bar. Prices are lower than other more conventional venues in the city.
🔢 K1 ✉ Via Sammartini 30, 20125 ☎ 02 6671 1370 🚇 Centrale FS

ITALIAN GRAND PRIX

The Italian Grand Prix at Monza ranks alongside Monte Carlo as one of the glitziest Grands Prix on the Formula 1 circuit. Plenty of stars and models watch the race under a sea of red Ferrari flags. Ticket information can be found on the website.
🔢 Off map to north ✉ Parco di Monza, 20052 Monza ☎ 039 248 2212; www.monzanet.it 🕐 Sep 🚉 From Stazione Centrale

Restaurants

PRICES

Prices are approximate, based on a 3-course meal for one person.
€€€   over €50
€€   €20–€50
€   under €20

AIMO E NADIA (€€€)

www.aimoenadia.com
Central Italian cuisine, cooked by award-winning chef Signor Aimo and his wife, Nadia. Every dish is a masterpiece, served in intimate surroundings. Tempts the senses of sight, smell and taste.
✚ Off map at A7 ✉ Via Montecuccoli 6, 20147 ☎ 02 416 886 ⏰ Mon–Fri lunch, dinner; Sat dinner only
🚇 Primaticcio

AL PONT DE FERR (€–€€)

Traditional *osteria* with brick archways and heavy wood panelling. Try the vegetable crepes with cheese.
✚ E8 ✉ Ripa di Porta Ticinese 55, 20143 ☎ 02 8940 6277 ⏰ Tue–Sun lunch, dinner 🚇 Porta Genova

ASSO DI FIORI (€€)

www.assodifiori.com
Attractive traditional restaurant by the canal, dedicated to cheese, cheese and more cheese! But delicious desserts, too.
✚ E8 ✉ Alzaia Naviglio Grande 54, 20144 ☎ 02 8940 9415 ⏰ Mon–Sat lunch, dinner; Sun dinner only
🚇 Porta Genova

CHANDELIER (€€)

www.chandelier.it
Real innovative fare made from a simple fusion of quality, fresh ingredients. Bright young things and arty types make up the majority of the clientele.
✚ L3 ✉ Via Giuseppe Broggi 17, 20129 ☎ 02 2024 0458 ⏰ Tue–Sat dinner only
🚇 Lima

COPACABANA (€€€)

www.copacabanaristorante.it
Milan's only dedicated Brazilian restaurant, with a Copacabana atmosphere. Giant ribs, steaks, oxtail and thick stews are served with black beans, spicy rice and salads.
✚ Off map at F1 ✉ Via Tartini 13, 20122 ☎ 02 3931 3142 ⏰ Daily, dinner only
🚇 Repubblica; then trolleybus 82 in the direction of Via Giovan Battista Varè

ETHNIC VARIETY

It has taken some years for international and ethnic cuisine to take hold in Milan—despite the fact that large numbers of immigrants moved to the city for work during the economic expansion of the 1980s. The Milanese have remained loyal to the traditional Italian cuisine, but gradually a more cosmopolitan attitude to food is coming to the fore. You can find fine restaurants cooking up dishes from Asia, South America and North Africa.

DA GASPARE (€€)

www.ristorantedagaspare.com
Despite refreshingly low prices, Da Gaspare stands head and shoulders above the rest of Milan's fish restaurants. Lobster, mussels, crab and more crustaceans. Tasty desserts, too. Small, uncomfortable and often noisy, but the regulars keep flooding back.
✚ B5 ✉ Via Carlo Ravizza 19 20149 ☎ 02 4800 6409 ⏰ Thu–Tue lunch, dinner
🚇 Buonarroti

EL BRELLÍN (€€)

www.brellini.it
Atmospheric restaurant in an attractive former grocery and wash-house beside the canal. Typical Milanese cooking and good wine list. Try the Sunday brunch.
✚ E8 ✉ Alzaia Naviglio Grande 14, 20144 ☎ 02 5810 1351 ⏰ Mon–Sat lunch, dinner; Sun brunch only
🚇 Porta Genova

IL SAMBUCO (€€€)

www.ilsambuco.it
One of the best restaurants in Milan, in the elegant Hermitage Hotel (▷ 112) in the north of the city. Fish and seafood are among the house specials, but it is equally renowned for its steak and its regional dishes. Warm, inviting, elegant dining room.
✚ E2 ✉ Via Messina 10, 20154 ☎ 02 3361 0333 ⏰ Mon–Sat lunch, dinner
🚇 Garibaldi 🚋 Tram 14

LA BOTTEGA DEL GELATO (€€)

This *gelateria*, not far from the central station, has been in business since the mid-19th century. Delicious ice cream, including peach, passion fruit, melon and tamarillo.
➕ L2 ✉ Via Pergolesi 3, 20124 ☎ 02 2940 0076
🕐 Thu–Tue 🚇 Caiazzo

LA COZZERIA (€)

www.lacozzeria.it
Each dish here is based upon a kilogram (about 2lb) of mussels. Chefs curry them, pepper them, make them into a soup or serve them with cream, spices or liqueurs.
➕ L8 ✉ Via Muratori 7, 20135 ☎ 02 5410 7164
🕐 Tue–Sun lunch, dinner; Mon dinner only 🚇 Porta Romana

LE VIGNE (€€)

There is a lot of hustle and bustle at this rustic *osteria* on the canalside. It does get very crowded but it's worth waiting for a table to sample the excellent food, especially the stews.
➕ E8 ✉ Ripa di Porta Ticinese 61, 20143 ☎ 02 837 5617 🕐 Mon–Sat lunch, dinner 🚇 Porta Genova

LOCANDO GRECO (€€)

Milan's oldest Greek restaurant overlooks a canal. Traditional dishes, such as *tzatziki* and *moussaka*, well prepared.
➕ E8 ✉ Via Ripa Ticinese 69, 20143 ☎ 02 5810 1834
🕐 Mon–Sat dinner only
🚇 Porta Genova

MAURO IL BOLOGNESE (€€)

A wealth of dishes from Bologna, the city known to Italians as 'the fat' for its wonderful, rich food. Every dish bursts with seasonal delights, such as mushrooms, truffles, soft fruit or tomatoes. Go when you feel really hungry.
➕ D9 ✉ Via Lombardini 14, 20143 ☎ 02 837 2866
🕐 Tue–Sun lunch, dinner
🚇 Romolo

ORSI (€€)

This *gelateria* down by the canal wins in summer with its nice terrace. The variety of ices is impressive—blueberry and zabaglione to name just two.
➕ F9 ✉ Via Torricelli 19, 20136 ☎ 02 8940 6807
🕐 Tue–Sun 🚇 Romolo

THE BILL

The bill (check), *il conto*, usually includes extras such as *servizio* (service). Iniquitous cover charges (*pane e coperto*) have now been outlawed, but some restaurants still try to get round the regulations. Only pay for bread (*pane*) if you have asked for it. Proper receipts–not a scrawled piece of paper–must be given by law. If you receive a scrap of paper, which is more likely in a pizzeria, and have doubts about the total, be sure to ask for a proper receipt (*una fattura* or *una ricevuta*).

PONTE ROSSO (€€)

Not your typical trattoria—this one is smart with a trendy orange and black interior, and looks more like a French bistro. Simple home-cooked Italian food like *mamma* used to make.
➕ E8 ✉ Ripa di Porta Ticinese 23, 20143 ☎ 02 837 3132 🕐 Tue–Sat lunch, dinner; Mon dinner only
🚇 Porta Genova

SPICE (€)

For a change from pizza and pasta, try this Thai restaurant a little north-east of central Milan.
➕ C3 ✉ Via Ippolito Nievo 33, 20145 ☎ 02 341 290
🕐 Mon–Sat lunch, dinner
🚇 Pagano, Buonarroti

TRADIZIONALE (€)

www.latradizionale.com
This busy pizzeria, in the canal area, is furnished with Milanese antiques. Not just delicious pizza, but fish and pasta, too. Reservations are advised.
➕ F8 ✉ Ripa di Porta Ticinese 7, 20123 ☎ 02 839 5133 🕐 Thu–Tue lunch, dinner; Wed dinner only
🚇 Porta Genova

UNCO (€–€€)

The name is short for Unconventional Restaurant, and so it is! Small morsels of a host of international tastes—from India to Mexico, Japan to South America,
➕ F9 ✉ Via Pavia 8, 20143 ☎ 02 5810 8230 🕐 Mon–Sat dinner 🚇 Porta Genova

There is a wide range of accommodation in Milan. Choose from world-class deluxe hotels in historic buildings, ultra-chic boutique hotels or family-run smaller hotels that haven't changed much in 30 years.

Introduction

You'll find the full range of hotel options in Milan as you would in any prosperous city. Prices can be steep, as establishments in the upper price range outnumber inexpensive options.

Best to Book

Although Milan has plenty of accommodation, the city is a major commercial hub with a constant flow of business people, so you will need to book in advance—especially if there is a trade fair or fashion show taking place at the same time. As there tends to be more commercial visitors than tourists, Milan's hotels are usually more in demand during the week, leaving more rooms available on weekends and hotels may drop their prices. As a large proportion of the hotels are located in clusters on the perimeter areas around the city, it can be difficult to secure a place to stay right in the *centro* without paying high prices.

Saving Money

Agree on a price before you make your reservation. Hotels often quote their most expensive price: ask if they have a cheaper room available. Sometimes they offer reduced weekend rates. Smaller hotels can be open to gentle bargaining, particularly during quieter times. Some hotels are willing to put another bed in a room for an extra 35 per cent, ideal for families. Rates vary according to season, sometimes as much as 25 per cent, and increase dramatically when there are trade events taking place.

TIPS

● If you haven't booked in advance, the local visitor information office will have lists and may be willing to make reservations for you.

● It's perfectly acceptable to ask to see the room before you decide to stay somewhere.

● You will be asked to leave your passport at reception. Don't forget it when you leave.

● Check-out time is normally 11am–12, but hotels will usually store your luggage till the end of the day.

All the comforts and modern facilities can be found in Milanese hotels

Budget Hotels

Hotel Aristmells

GRITTI
www.hotelgritti.com
Close to the Duomo in a quiet square, this hotel has a very pleasant atmosphere. Its 48 rooms are well equipped, all with a bath and shower, minibar, and hair dryer.
➕ G6 ✉ Piazza Santa Maria Beltrade 4, 20123 ☎ 02 801 056; fax 02 8901 0999
🚇 Duomo

HOTEL CASA MIA 〉
www.casamiahotel.it
This is a good choice if your budget does not stretch to a four-star. It is in a decent location close to the metro, with very friendly, helpful staff and the 15 rooms are extremely clean.
➕ J3 ✉ Viale Vittorio Veneto 30, 20124 ☎ 02 657 5249; fax 02 655 2228
🚇 Repubblica

HOTEL DUE GIARDINI
www.hotelduegiardini.it ⁊
Excellent value hotel near Stazione Centrale. No ⁿ⁰ elevator but staff are on hand to help with lug- in/○ gage. All rooms have modern comforts and private bathrooms. Breakfast is served in the garden when weather permits.
➕ K2 ✉ Via Benedetto Marcello 47, 20124 ☎ 02 2952 1093; fax 02 2951 6933
🚇 Centrale FS

LONDON HOTEL
www.hotel-london-milan.com
You get a warm welcome at this central hotel, where the comfy lounge is a popular place to gather. Overlooking a tranquil back street, the 30 large rooms are spartan and slightly dated.
➕ G5 ✉ Via Rovello 3, 20121 ☎ 02 7202 0166; fax 02 805 7037 🚇 Cairoli
€130

NUOVO
www.hotelnuovomilano.com
Good value for a central location. All 36 rooms are clean and compact and most have telephone, television and, some, a private bathroom. It can be noisy at night.
➕ H6 ✉ Piazza Beccaria Cesare 6, 20122 ☎ 02 8646 4444; fax 02 7200 1752
🚇 San Babila

ROVELLO
www.hotel-rovello.it
Intimate hotel with just

10 rooms, midway between the Duomo and Parco Sempione. Full of character, the rooms have wooden floors and beams, and overlook a courtyard.
➕ G5 ✉ Via Rovello 18, 20121 ☎ 02 8646 4654; fax 02 720 3656 🚇 Cairoli

SAN FRANCISCO
www.hotel-sanfrancisco.it/sito/
This family-run hotel close to Giardini Pubblici has 31 simple rooms and a small, beautiful garden. Warm and welcoming staff.
➕ Off map at M1 ✉ Viale Lombardia 55, 20131 ☎ 02 236 0302; fax 02 2668 0377
🚇 Piola   €63

SPERONARI
A few minutes' walk from Galleria Vittorio Emanuele. The 24 rooms are small and basic but clean and tidy—some have a private bathroom. You will find that during trade fairs the hotel fills up with business guests.
➕ G6 ✉ Via Speronari 4, 20123 ☎ 02 8646 1125; fax 02 7200 3178 🚇 Duomo

VECCHIA MILANO
www.hotelvecchiamilano.it
In a peaceful street just off Via Torino, this charming hotel has an air of Italian antiquity. The 43 spacious rooms have old-fashioned features such as period taps and ancient portraits.
➕ F6 ✉ Via Borromei 4, 20123 ☎ 02 875 042; fax 02 8645 4292 🚇 Duomo

Mid-Range Hotels

PRICES

Expect to pay between €160 and €350 per night for a mid-range hotel.

ANTICA LOCANDA LEONARDO

www.anticalocandaleonardo.com

Comfort and refinement in a peaceful atmosphere. The rooms have been recently renovated, and are individually furnished, from an authentic antique style to a more classic style, while the walls are adorned with works of art by contemporary artists. During good weather, take advantage of the pretty internal garden.

➕ E5 ✉ Corso Magenta 78, 20123 ☎ 02 4801 4197; fax 02 4801 9012 🚇 Cadorna

ANTICA LOCANDA SOLFERINO

www.anticalocandasolferino.it

Tucked away in a quiet cobbled street, this delightful old-fashioned *pensione* is very friendly. The simple but spacious rooms, decorated with antiques and chintz curtains, have pretty balconies. There are only 11 rooms, so book in advance.

➕ H3 ✉ Via Castelfidardo 2, 20121 ☎ 02 657 0129 🚇 Moscova

BAVIERA

www.hotelbaviera.com

Comfortable if slightly behind the times, this extremely gracious hotel considers itself a business person's hotel. A pleasant, updated lounge has restful sofas and wooden floors. The 50 bedrooms vary in size and have old-fashioned bedding. Within walking distance of Stazione Centrale.

➕ K3 ✉ Via Castaldi 7, 20124 ☎ 02 659 0551; fax 02 2900 3281 🚇 Repubblica

BRISTOL

www.hotelbristolmil.it

Exit the Milano Centrale station via the stairs and you'll find yourself at the front door of this classic hotel. A refined Anglo-French style blends with modern amenities, which

PRICES

Italian hotels charge for the room not for each person. The price, by law, should be displayed in the room itself and may or may not include breakfast. Prices for different rooms often vary within a hotel, so if a room is too expensive be sure to ask if another is available for less (you may well be shown the most expensive first). Single rooms are in short supply and can cost nearly as much as a double room. Hotels in Milan are expensive, but they are generally of a good standard. It is best to book well in advance, particularly if there is a fashion show or trade fair taking place at the time.

include 68 soundproofed rooms and in-room Jacuzzis and Internet facilities. Helpful English-speaking staff.

➕ K1 ✉ Via Scarlatti 32, 20124 ☎ 02 669 4141; fax 02 670 2942 🚇 Repubblica

CANADA

www.canadahotel.it

What this glass structure lacks in character it makes up for with 35 pristine, modern rooms that will meet all your needs. There are good views of the Duomo from the eighth floor. About a 10-minute walk from the *centro storico*.

➕ H7 ✉ Via Santa Sofia 16, 20122 ☎ 02 5830 4844; fax 02 5830 0282 🚇 Crocetta

CARLYLE BRERA

www.carlylebrerahotel.com

The stylish Carlyle Brera, in the Brera district, is a cut above most business hotels. It provides free bicycles to use around town and a high-class buffet breakfast. Very near to the metro station. 94 rooms.

➕ G3 ✉ Corso Garibaldi 84, 20121 ☎ 02 2900 3888; fax 02 2900 3993 🚇 Moscova

CAVOUR

www.hotelcavour.it

In an ideal spot between La Scala and the Giardini Pubblici, this friendly hotel's 113 large rooms are decorated in cream with light-wood panels and have satellite TV and air-conditioning.

H4 ✉ Via Fatebenefratelli 21, 20121 ☎ 02 620 001; fax 02 659 2263 🚇 Turati

GRAN DUCA DI YORK
www.ducadiyork.com
Housed in a grand 18th-century building, within a short distance of Piazza Duomo and the Pinacoteca Ambrosiana. Newly renovated in 2004, the standard rooms are plain but very comfortable—there are superior rooms available; ask for one of the four rooms with a terrace.
G6 ✉ Via Moneta 1, 20123 ☎ 02 874 863; fax 02 869 0344 🚇 Cordusio

KING
www.hotelkingmilano.com
Housed in a lovely *palazzo* in a lively central location, this pleasant hotel has an opulent lobby with period furniture, 48 comfortable rooms and efficient, courteous staff.
F5 ✉ Via Corso Magenta 19, 20123 ☎ 02 874 432; fax 02 8901 0798 🚇 Cadorna

MANIN
www.hotelmanin.it
A sophisticated, modern hotel on the edge of the prestigious shopping streets and opposite Giardini Pubblici. The huge conservatory-cum-garden area is ideal for lunch or a cocktail. Nicely decorated throughout, with 118 spacious bedrooms; some with terrace or balcony overlooking the gardens.
J3 ✉ Via Manin 7, 20121

02 659 6511; fax 02 655 2160 🚇 Turati

MANZONI
www.hotelmanzoni.com
This was always the poor relation among the designer boutiques of the Quad d'Oro, but after closure for a revamp and overhaul, its opening in 2007 should see it more on a par with its local environment.
H5 ✉ Via Santo Spirito 20, 20124 ☎ 02 7600 5700; fax 02 784 212 🚇 Montenapoleone

HOTEL MICHELANGELO
www.milanhotel.it
Convenient for transport to Milan's two major airports as Stazione Centrale is visible from the hotel. Many of the 300 bedrooms have a Jacuzzi and other mod

BOOKING

Hotel information is available from the tourist office on Via Marconi and at the "Passaggi" agency in the Central Station. Or try these hotel booking agencies:
CPHI 'HotelMe' ☎ Toll-free in Italy 800 015772; outside Italy 02 29531605, www.hotelme.it
Easy Hotel ☎ 02 2940 4099
Centro Prenotazioni Nazionale ☎ Toll-free 800 008777, www.initalia.it
Hotel To Book www.hotel-milan-tobook.com

cons all surrounded by a gleaming wooden finish.
K1 ✉ Via Scarlatti 33, 20124 ☎ 02 67551; fax 02 669 4232 🚇 Centrale FS

REGINA
www.hotelregina.it
A charming 18th-century mansion adorned with antique furniture and paintings. The 43 rooms have an old-fashioned appeal, with parquet floors and large rugs. Near the Navigli canals. Pretty garden.
F7 ✉ Via Cesare Correnti 13, 20123 ☎ 02 5810 6913; fax 02 5810 7033 🚇 Missori

SIR EDWARD
www.hotelsiredward.it
Maximum comfort in the heart of the *centro storico*, just around the corner from the Duomo. The 40 elegant rooms feature whirlpool baths and are equipped for all business people's needs. Very courteous staff.
G6 ✉ Via Mazzini 4, 20123 ☎ 02 877 877; fax 02 877 844 🚇 Duomo

SPADARI AL DUOMO
www.spadarihotel.com
A small hotel with contemporary art and sculpture displayed against vivid blue decoration. The 39 spacious bedrooms have designer furniture and each has a Jacuzzi. No restaurant, but snacks are served. A few steps from Teatro alla Scala.
G6 ✉ Via Spadari 11, 20123 ☎ 02 7200 2371; fax 02 286 1184 🚇 Duomo

Luxury Hotels

FOUR SEASONS

www.fourseasons.com/milan
A beautifully restored 15th-century monastery in the Quad d'Oro set around a cloistered courtyard. The huge opulent reception has frescoes, columns and vaults, and the 118 spacious bedrooms are stylish.
 H5 ✉ Via Gesù 6/8, 21021 ☎ 02 770 88; fax 02 7708 5000 Ⓜ Montenapoleone

GRAND HOTEL DE MILAN

www.grandhoteletdemilan.it
The Grand has an enviable position, right next door to La Scala. For 150 years the Grand has opened its doors to royals and celebrities. The hotel oozes distinction, with staff buzzing around the ornate foyer catering to guests' every need. The 77 rooms have period decoration, yet the hotel's facilities are firmly 21st century.
H4 ✉ Via Manzoni 29, 20121 ☎ 02 723 141; fax 02 8646 0861 Ⓜ Montenapoleone

THE GRAY

www.hotelthegray.com
Facing the renowned Galleria, this stylish hotel is minimalist design at its best: dim lighting and metallic decoration with a splash of red. Framed prints and modern lights enhance the 21 rooms, all with the latest mod cons including DVDs and hydro tubs.
H5 ✉ Via San Raffaele 6, 20121 ☎ 02 720 8951; fax 02 866 526 Ⓜ Duomo

HERMITAGE

www.monrifhotels.it
A refined hotel out near the Cimitero Monumentale with 131 bright, spacious rooms, all furnished in dark wood. Restaurant Il Sambuco is said to be one of the best in Milan (▷ 105).
E2 ✉ Via Messina 10, 20154 ☎ 02 318 170; fax 02 3310 7399 Ⓜ Garibaldi

PRINCIPE DI SAVOIA

www.hotelprincipedisavoia.com
Meticulous gardens leading up to a majestic white façade give an indication of the sumptuous interior you are about to enter. With a 1930s feel, the rooms are adorned with antiques, marble and luxury carpets. The 404 bedrooms are a generous size. Indoor pool and health suite.
J3 ✉ Piazza della Repubblica 17, 20124 ☎ 02 62301; fax 02 659 5838 Ⓜ Repubblica

SHERATON DIANA MAJESTIC

www.sheraton.com/dianamajestic
Set in pretty gardens, close to Milan's main shopping area, this art deco hotel is the place to be seen; it is popular during fashion shows with models and journalists. The circular foyer has leather chairs and period furniture, and the 107 Imperial-style rooms have elegant marble bathrooms.
K4 ✉ Viale Piave 42, 20129 ☎ 02 20581; fax 02 2058 2058 Ⓜ Porta Venezia

STRAF

www.straf.it
Unconventional modern comfort in a prime spot next to the Duomo. An ultra-sleek minimalist look has been created using innovative materials such as raw concrete, iron, slate, burnished brass, gauze-effect glass and scratched mirrors. 64 rooms.
H5 ✉ Via San Raffaele 3, 20121 ☎ 02 805 081; fax 02 8909 5294 Ⓜ Duomo

Need to Know

Planning Ahead

When to Go

Milan is primarily a business destination, with little seasonal variation in the number of visitors or cost of hotels, but avoid visiting during major events, such as fashion shows. April, May, June and September are good months to visit. June begins to get hot and it cools off at the end of September when there are increasing bouts of rain.

> **TIME**
>
> Italy is one hour ahead of GMT, six hours ahead of New York and nine hours ahead of Los Angeles.

AVERAGE DAILY MAXIMUM TEMPERATURES											
JAN	FEB	MAR	APR	MAY	JUN	JUL	AUG	SEP	OCT	NOV	DEC
43°F	46°F	54°F	59°F	68°F	73°F	79°F	79°F	70°F	61°F	54°F	45°F
6°C	8°C	12°C	15°C	20°C	23°C	26°C	26°C	21°C	16°C	12°C	7°C

Spring (March to May) is very pleasant, although rain can persist into May.

Summer (June to August) high temperatures bring a humid haze and normally some thunderstorms, which help to clear the air.

Autumn (September to November) gradually turns from showers to heavy rain, and November is dank and wet.

Winter (December to February) Alpine winds make it very cold and there can be heavy frosts and thick fog. December can produce pleasant bright, crisp days.

WHAT'S ON

January *Corteo dei Re Magi* (6 Jan): A Nativity-themed procession travels from the Duomo to Sant'Eustorgio.

February *Carnevale Ambrosiano*: The carnival culminates with a parade on the first Saturday of Lent.

March MODIT-*Milanovendemodo* (early Mar): International fashion show.

Milano–SanRemo (third Sat): Milan hosts the start of this famous international bicycle race.

April *Fiera dei Fiori* (Mon after Easter): Fair devoted to flower growing, near the Sant'Angelo Franciscan convent.

Stramilano (early Apr): Annual marathon race with over 50,000 competitors.

June *Festa del Naviglio* (first Sun): Festival held along the Navigli canals; concerts, street performers, sports, handicrafts and regional cooking.

July/August *Festival Latino-Americano*: Festival of Latin-American music, handicrafts and cuisine.

September *Gran Premio di Monza*: Formula One Grand Prix of Italy.

October MODIT-*Milanovendemoda* (early Oct): second major fashion show.

December *Mercato di Sant'Ambrogio* (7 Dec): Festival celebrating Sant'Ambrogio, Milan's 4th-century patron saint and the city's first mayor. Stalls are set up around the church of Sant'Ambrogio and most people take the day off work to attend the market. Also called *Oh Bej! Oh Bej!* after the children's cries of delight in the 16th century.

Milan Online

www.milaninfotourist.com
Milan's official website includes practical information on city sights, accommodation, restaurants, entertainment, events, guided tours, transportation and lots more. Updated regularly.

www.hellomilano.it
English site that is easy to understand and has good up-to-date details on what's on, news, restaurants, nightlife, shopping and general information.

www.enit.it
The main Italian Tourist Board website carries a wealth of information about the whole country—available in several languages.

www.emmeti.it
An Italy-based site, in English and Italian, with a good range of information on Milan and links to other sites. It's strong on local events and offers an online hotel booking service.

www.initaly.com
An enthusiastic site run by passionate lovers of Italy from the US. It's packed with information and articles about the country, with quirky tips and insider stories, and makes excellent browsing when you're planning your trip.

www.hotelme.it
A user-friendly hotel booking service, with good coverage of Milan. Previous visitors share opinions and tips. English version available.

www.ticketweb.prenofacile.it
Buy your tickets for nearly every event going on in Milan—theatre, music, sport, exhibitions.

www.apt.pv.it/www.aptcremona.it/ www.apt.bergamo/www.lakecomo.com
Official websites for Pavia, Cremona, Bergamo and Lake Como. All have English versions.

PRIME TRAVEL SITES

www.atm-mi.it
Milan's city transport system runs this informative site, where you'll find everything you could possibly want to know, including timetables, maps and how to buy the best ticket for your needs— Italian and English.

www.trenitalia.it
The official site of the Italian State Railways, with excellent train information.

www.fodors.com
A complete travel-planning site. You can research prices and weather; book air tickets, cars and rooms; pose questions (and get answers) to fellow travellers; and find links to other sites.

CYBERCAFÉS

Gr@zianet
Large café with plenty of computers just outside Stazione Centrale.
✉ Piazza Duca d'Aosta 14, 20124 ☎ No phone
🕓 Daily 8am–midnight
💶 €2 for 20 minutes

Mondadori
Inside Mondadori Multicentre—a music, book and software megastore.
✉ Via Marghera 28, 20129
☎ No phone 🕓 Tue–Sat 10am–midnight 💶 €3 for 1 hour

Getting There

VISAS AND PASSPORTS

For the latest passport and visa information, look up the British embassy website at www.britishembassy.gov.uk or the United States embassy at www.americanembassy.com/europe. EU citizens can obtain reduced-cost health care with the production of the EHIC card. However, full health and travel insurance is strongly advised.

CUSTOMS REGULATIONS

EU nationals do not have to declare goods imported for their personal use.
The limits for non-EU visitors are 200 cigarettes or 100 small cigars or 250g of tobacco; 1 litre of alcohol (over 22 per cent alcohol) or 2 litres of fortified wine; 50g of perfume.

AIRPORTS

There are direct flights from all over the world into Malpensa airport, Milan's main international gateway, while Linate airport, classed as a city airport, handles just Italian domestic and European flights. Visitors from Europe can also arrive by rail or by bus.

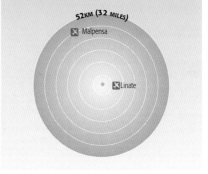

52KM (32 MILES)

Malpensa

Linate

FROM MALPENSA

Most flights arrive at Malpensa, 50km (31 miles) northwest of the city (☎ 02 7845 2200; www.sea-aeroportimilano.it). The Malpensa Express train (☎ 02 20222, www.fnmgroup.it/www.lenord.it) runs to Cadorna–Ferrovie Nord (every 30 minutes, 6.53am–9.53pm, 10.23pm on Sun; €11, journey time 40 minutes). You need to stamp your ticket in the machine located on the platform before boarding the train. The Malpensa Bus Express (☎ 02 240 7954) leaves from outside the terminal to Stazione Centrale (every 30 minutes, 5.15am–10.35pm; €5.50, journey time 50–60 minutes). Malpensa Shuttle (☎ 02 5858 3185) operates a shuttle bus to Stazione Centrale (every 20 minutes, 5am–11.15pm; €5, journey time 50–60 minutes). Taxis to the city can take up to 75 minutes depending on the traffic and are expensive (€75). Make sure you get an official white taxi. If someone approaches you offering a taxi be aware this will cost you more. Taxis returning to Malpensa should display a sticker 'taxi autorizzato per il servizio aeroportuale lombardo' on the screen.

FROM LINATE

Linate, the closest airport, is only 6km (4 miles) east of the city (☎ 02 7845 2200; www.sea-aeroportimilano.it). The most convenient option for getting into the city is by taxi; official white cabs line up outside the terminal (€20–€25, but check the cost before). ATM city bus No. 73 (every 20 minutes, 5.35am–12.35am; journey time 25 minutes) goes to Piazza San Babila (tickets €1 from vending machines). STAM coach service run a service to Stazione Centrale (every 30 minutes, 5.40am–9.35pm; €2; journey time 25 minutes).

ARRIVING BY BUS

The majority of domestic and international buses arrive at the main terminus in Piazza Castello. Autostradale Viaggi is the major bus company connecting Milan with the rest of Italy.

ARRIVING BY CAR

It is not advisable to drive into Central Milan. The city is divided into segments with a one-way system and you can only enter the city at a limited number of points. The 'Sosta Milano' parking system is extremely difficult to under-stand and unless you have parking at your hotel it is really better not to use a car. If you do bring a car be aware that fuel stations in the city close for lunch, on Saturday afternoons and all day Sunday. Do not leave your car on yellow lines or in areas marked by a tow-away symbol. The bottom line is you are far better off using the excellent public transport system.

ARRIVING BY RAIL

Most international and domestic trains arrive at Stazione Centrale, in the northeast of the city, although the Malpensa Express arrives at Cardona–Ferrovie Nord, closer to the city cen-tre. There are easy connections to the rest of the city from here: The station is on Metro lines 2 and 3, taxis line up outside the entrance, and several trams and buses stop right outside.

HANDY HINT

In the land of the Vespa, it's tempting to hire a scooter (*motorino*) and Milan has many scooter rental outlets. But scooters are not for the faint-hearted, and if you've never ridden one in a big city, Milan is not the place to start.

CONSULATES

● **British Consulate**
✉ Via San Paulo 7
☎ 02 723 001
🕐 Mon–Fri 9.15–12.15, 2.15–3.45

● **US Consulate**
✉ Via Principe Amedeo 2/10
☎ 02 290 351
🕐 Mon–Fri 9–12

Getting Around

Milan has an efficient integrated transportation system comprising trams, buses and a Metro, which is easy to use (www.atm-mi.it).

BUSES AND TRAMS

Bus and tram routes cover the whole city and also follow the Metro routes overground. Both are very efficient and run approximately every 10 minutes. They can get very crowded, especially during rush hour, so take care of your belongings. Bus and tram stops have a yellow sign displaying the route and a timetable. All buses and trams in Milan are orange except for the tourist trams, which are one of the best ways of seeing the city.

THE METRO

The Metro is the easiest and fastest option, though you may have to combine it with a bus or tram. The Metro consists of four lines: red MM1, green MM2, yellow MM3 and blue *passante ferroviario* (suburban loop). These intersect at the hub stations of Stazione Centrale, Duomo, Cardorna and Loreto.

TICKETS

Tickets must be purchased in advance and stamped in a machine once on board. Fines are handed out to anyone caught without a ticket. A single (€1) is valid for 75 minutes from validation and can be used on the entire system for as many bus and tram trips as you want, plus one Metro journey. One- and two-day travel cards (€3/€5.50) are also available. These last 24/48 hours respectively from time of first stamping; once stamped you do not need to do it again. Tickets are sold at tobacconists, bars, newsstands, tourist offices and Metro stations. The network runs 6am–midnight, with night buses continuing until 1.30am.

TAXIS

Official taxis in Milan are normally white and the charges are reasonable. It is almost impossible to hail a passing cab so it's best to call

(Radiotaxi ☎ 02 4040; 02 8585; 02 4000; 02 6969) when you want one—they usually arrive quite quickly—or go to a taxi rank (stand) at Piazza del Duomo, Stazione Centrale, Piazza della Scala, Piazza San Babila, Piazza Diaz and Via Manzoni.

SCOOTERS, MOPEDS AND BICYCLES

Even experienced riders or cyclists should be careful if using this mode of transport on Milan's congested roads. There are several places in the city that hire these forms of transport: try Bianco Blu (✉ Via Gallarate 33 ☎ 02 3082 2430; www.biancoblu.com) for scooters and mopeds; AWS (✉ Via Ponte Seveso 33 ☎ 02 6707 2145) for bicycles.

WALKING

Walking is the best way to get around Milan, but do beware of chaotic traffic when crossing the road.

ORGANIZED SIGHTSEEING

A bus tour, run by Autostradale, leaves Piazza Duomo (Tue–Sun 9.30am) for a three-hour tour to most of Milan's main sights, accompanied by a multilingual commentary; cost €50 including pick-up and drop-off at selected hotels and entrance fees. For a fascinating overview of the city take the City Sightseeing Milano bus (02 867 131; www.city-sightseeing.it)— two different hop-on hop-off guided tours with multilingual recorded commentary. It departs from Piazza Castello (daily all year; tours leave from between 10am and 6.45) and lasts for about 1 hour 15 minutes; cost €15; reduced cost for children (5–15 years) €7. You can buy tickets for both tours at the tourist information offices.
An alternative is to view the city on foot. Tourist Guide of Milan (Via Marconi 1 ☎ 02 8645 0433) offers themed tours by expert guides. A Friend in Milan (☎ 02 2952 0570; www.friendinmilan.co.uk) is another organization that provides guided walking tours throughout the city.

Essential Facts

MONEY

The euro (€) is the official currency of Italy. Banknotes are in denominations of 5, 10, 20, 50, 100, 200 and 500 euros, and coins in denominations of 1, 2, 5, 10, 20, 50 cents and 1 and 2 euros. Credit cards are widely accepted and most banks have ATMs.

10 euros

50 euros

200 euros

500 euros

WOMEN VISITORS

● Women are generally safe visiting alone in Milan.
● After dark avoid Parco Sempione, the rail station and poorly lit streets away from the middle of the city.

ELECTRICITY

● Voltage is 220 volts and sockets take two round pins.

LOST PROPERTY

● Council lost property office ⊠ Via Friuli 30 ☎ 02 8845 3907/8 🕑 Mon–Fri 8.30–4
● Central railway left luggage office ⊠ Stazione Centrale (1st floor of Galleria Partenze) ☎ 02 6371 2667 🕑 Daily 6am–1am.
● It is imperative to report losses of passports to the police (▷ Emergency Numbers panel opposite).

MAIL

● General post office information 803 160; www.poste.it
● Main post office ⊠ Via Cordusio 4 ☎ 02 7248 2126 🕑 Mon–Fri 8–7, Sat 8.30–12
● There is another big post office at the Stazione Centrale ⊠ Via Sammartini ☎ 02 6749 3748 🕑 Mon–Fri 8–7, Sat 8.30–12.30
● You can buy stamps (*francobolli*) from post offices or from tobacconists displaying a white T sign on a dark background.
● Post boxes are small, red and marked *Poste* or *Lettere*. The slot on the left is for addresses within the city and the slot on the right is for other destinations.

MEDICINES AND MEDICAL TREATMENT

● Medical emergencies ☎ 118 or go to the *Pronto Soccorso* (casualty department or emergency room) of the nearest hospital.
● Poison Antidote Centre ☎ 02 6610 1029
● Pharmacies are indicated by a large green or red cross.
● There is a free emergency number giving details of your nearest pharmacy ☎ 800 801 185. 24-hour pharmacy: Farmacia della Stazione Centrale ☎ 02 669 0935
● There are several night pharmacies, including those located in: Piazza Duomo 21 ☎ 02 287 8668; Via Boccaccio 26 ☎ 02 469 5281; Corso Magenta ☎ 02 4800 6772

OPENING TIMES
● Banks: Mon–Fri 8.30–1.30, 3–4
● Post offices: Mon–Fri 8.30–1.50, Sat 8–12
The main city post offices stay open at
lunchtime and close at 7
● Shops: normally 9.30–1, 3.30–7.30
● Museums: see individual entries.
● Churches: 7 or 8–12.30, 3 or 4–7.30
Main tourist attractions often stay open longer.
No two are the same.

PUBLIC HOLIDAYS
1 Jan: New Year's Day; 6 Jan: Epiphany; Easter
Sunday; Easter Monday; 25 Apr: Liberation Day;
1 May: Labour Day; 2 Jun: Republic Day; 15
Aug: Assumption; 1 Nov: All Saints' Day; 8 Dec:
Immaculate Conception; 25 Dec: Christmas
Day; 26 Dec: St. Stephen's Day. Most places
of interest close on New Year's Day, 1 May
and Christmas, while others close on all
public holidays.

TELEPHONES
● There are few telephone centres in the city:
Galleria Vittorio Emanuele II ☎ Daily
8am–9.30pm; Stazione Centrale ☎ Daily
9am–9.30pm.
● Phone cards (*carta, scheda or tessera
telefonica*) are the most practical way to use
a public phone as few public telephones
take coins.
● Directory Enquiries ☎ 12
● International directories ☎ 176
● International operator ☎ 170
● Cheap rate is all day Sunday and 9pm–8am
(national) on other days; 10pm–8am
(international).
● To call Italy from the UK, dial 00 followed by
39 (the code for Italy) then the number. To call
the UK from Italy dial 00 44 then drop the first
zero from the area code.
● To call Italy from the US dial 011 followed by
39. To call the US from Italy dial 00 1
● Milan's area code (02) must be dialled even
if you are calling from within the city.

NEWSPAPERS
The daily city newspaper, *Il
Corrière*, includes listings for
theatre, music and cinema.
Other Italian dailies, *La
Repubblica* and *Corriere
della Sera*, produce weekly
supplements with up-to-date
listings of cultural events in
the city. The tourist office has
two free magazines: *Milano
Giorno & Notte)*, in English,
giving information and listings on the arts, theatre,
nightlife and a little on shopping, and *Milanomese,* with
listings of what's on.
Foreign newspapers can usually be bought after about
2.30 on the day of issue from
booths (*edicole*) in the city.
European editions of the
Financial Times, USA Today
and *International Herald
Tribune* are also available.

Language

All Italian words are pronounced as written, with each vowel and consonant sounded. Only the letter *h* is silent, but it modifies the sound of other letters. The letter *c* is hard, as in English 'cat', except when followed by *i* or *e*, when it becomes the soft *ch* of 'cello'. Similarly, *g* is soft (as in the English 'giant') when followed by *i* or *e*–*giardino, gelati*; otherwise hard (as in 'gas')–*gatto*. Words ending in *o* are almost always masculine in gender (plural: *-i*); those ending in *a* are generally feminine (plural: *-e*). Use the polite second person (*lei*) to speak to strangers and the informal second person (*tu*) to friends or children.

USEFUL WORDS	
yes	*sì*
no	*no*
please	*per favore*
thank you	*grazie*
you're welcome	*prego*
excuse me! !	*scusi*
where	*dove*
here	*qui*
there	*là*
when	*quando*
now	*adesso*
later	*più tardi*
why	*perchè*
who	*chi*
may I/can I	*posso*
good morning	*buon giorno*
good afternoon/good evening	*buona sera/buona notte*
hello/goodbye (informal)	*ciao*
hello (on the telephone)	*pronto*
I'm sorry	*mi dispiace*
left/right	*sinistra/destra*
open/closed	*aperto/chiuso*
good/bad	*buono/cattivo*
big/small	*grande/piccolo*
with/without	*con/senza*
more/less	*più/meno*
hot/cold	*caldo/freddo*
early/late	*presto/ritardo*
now/later	*adesso/più tardi*
today/tomorrow	*oggi/domani*
when?/do you have?	*quando?/avete?*

NUMBERS	
1	*uno, una*
2	*due*
3	*tre*
4	*quattro*
5	*cinque*
6	*sei*
7	*sette*
8	*otto*
9	*nove*
10	*dieci*
20	*venti*
30	*trenta*
40	*quaranta*
50	*cinquanta*
100	*cento*
1,000	*mille*

EMERGENCIES

help!	aiuto!
stop, thief!	al ladro!
can you help me, please?	può aiutarmi, per favore?
call the police/an ambulance	chiami la polizia/ un'ambulanza
I have lost my wallet/ passport	ho perso il passaporto/ il portafoglio
where is the police station?	dov'è il commissariato?
where is the hospital?	dov'è l'ospedale?
I don't feel well	non mi sento bene
first aid	pronto soccorso

COLOURS

black	nero
brown	marrone
pink	rosa
red	rosso
orange	arancia
yellow	giallo
green	verde
light blue	celeste
sky blue	azzuro
purple	viola
white	bianco
grey	grigio

USEFUL PHRASES

how are you? (informal)	come sta/stai?
I'm fine	sto bene
I do not understand	non ho capito
how much is it?	quant'è?
do you have a room?	avete camere libere?
how much per night?	quanto costa una notte?
with bath/shower	con bagno/doccia
when is breakfast served?	a che ora è servita la colazione?
where is the train/ bus station?	dov'è la stazione ferroviaria degli autobus?
where are we?	dove siamo?
do I have to get off here?	devo scendere qui?
I'm looking for...	cerco...
where can I buy...?	dove posso comprare...?
a table for... please	un tavolo per... per favore
can I have the bill?	il conto
we didn't have this	non abbiamo avuto questo
where are the toilets?	dove sono i gabinetti?

DAYS/MONTHS

Monday	lunedì
Tuesday	martedì
Wednesday	mercoledì
Thursday	giovedì
Friday	venerdì
Saturday	sabato
Sunday	domenica
January	gennaio
February	febbraio
March	marzo
April	aprile
May	maggio
June	giugno
July	luglio
August	agosto
September	settembre
October	ottobre
November	novembre
December	dicembre

Timeline

NAPOLEON'S RULE

The city of Milan welcomed the arrival of Napoleon, and indeed it was he who brought forward the idea of the unification of Italy. His contributions to the city included reforming the educational and legal system, inaugurating the building of new public offices and establishing new museums and art galleries. He even saw the completion of the Duomo so he could hold his coronation there as the self-appointed 'king of Italy'. However, after 18 years of rule and high taxation the Milanese people were relieved when Napoleon was defeated at the Battle of Waterloo and Milan was returned to Habsburg rule.

$222BC$ The Romans defeat the Gauls. Milan becomes the most important city in the Western Roman Empire after Rome.

$AD374$ Sant'Ambrogio (St. Ambrose) becomes Bishop of Milan. The city flourishes.

452 The city is devastated by Attila the Hun, then again in 489 by the Goths.

568 Lombards invade and take power.

774 Rebirth of the city under the rule of Charlemagne.

1042 Milan becomes an autonomous city.

1162 German Emperor Frederick I invades. Milan is burned to the ground.

1176 Battle of Legnano gives independence to northern Italian cities.

1277 Rise of the Visconti family. The Duomo is commissioned in 1386.

1450 Rise of the Sforza family; for 50 years art and commerce flourish.

1499 Louis XII of France occupies Milan.

$1540–1706$ Milan under Spanish rule.

1706 Control of the city passes to the Austrian Habsburgs.

From left to right: Milan's awesome cathedral. Detail of a statue at the Castello Sforzesco. Relaxing in the grounds of the castle. Gloriously illuminated—the Duomo at night

1796–1814 Napoleonic rule. New building work is undertaken.

1804 Napoleon's coronation at the Duomo.

1815 Napoleon is defeated and Milan is handed back to the Habsburgs.

1848 Unification—Milan becomes part of Italy. The population increases to 240,000.

1919 Fascist movement founded by Benito Mussolini in Milan.

1939–1945 Milan suffers serious bomb damage during World War II.

1950s Milan leads Italy's economic recovery.

1960s Industrial and student unrest. Acts of terrorism take place.

1990s Corruption and political scandal rife; Milan becomes known as 'bribe' city.

2004 La Scala Opera House opens after three years of closure for restoration.

2006 The Prime Minister, Milanese Silvio Berlusconi, resigns in April. The Centre Left party under Romano Prodi leads the country.

2007 Romano Prodi's government is narrowly re-elected by the Senate after a vote of no confidence.

EARLY DAYS

During the Bronze Age, the Ligurians were the first to settle in the Po Valley, and by the sixth century BC the powerful Etruscans were well ensconced. By 338–386BC, after various skirmishes, the area was ruled by the Gauls.

SANT'AMBROGIO

The patron saint of Milan, whose feast day is on 7 December, was Bishop of Milan from AD374–397. As a result of his integrity and skill in negotiating between the Catholic and Arian church officials, Milan became an important religious hub.

Index

Milan's
25 Best

WRITTEN BY Jackie Staddon and Hilary Weston
DESIGN CONCEPT AND DESIGN WORK Kate Harling
COVER DESIGN Tigist Getachew
INDEXER Marie Lorimer
IMAGE RETOUCHING AND REPRO Sarah Butler
EDITORIAL MANAGEMENT Apostrophe S Limited
REVIEWING EDITOR Jacinta O'Halloran
SERIES EDITOR Paul Mitchell

ISBN 978-1-4000-1827-7

SECOND EDITION

IMPORTANT TIP
Time inevitably brings changes, so always confirm prices, travel facts, and other perishable information when it matters. Although Fodor's cannot accept responsibility for errors, you can use this guide in the confidence that we have taken every care to ensure its accuracy.

SPECIAL SALES
This book is available for special discounts for bulk purchases for sales promotions or premiums. Special editions, including personalized covers, excerpts of existing books, and corporate imprints, can be created in large quantities for special needs. For more information, write to Special Markets/Premium Sales, 1745 Broadway, MD 6–2, New York, NY 10019 or email specialmarkets@randomhouse.com.

Colour separation by Keenes
Printed and bound by Leo, China
10 9 8 7 6 5 4 3 2 1

A03143
Maps in this title produced from mapping © MAIRDUMONT / Falk Verlag 2007
Transport map © Communicarta Ltd, UK

The Automobile Association would like to thank the following photographers, companies and picture libraries for their assistance in the preparation of this book.

Abbreviations for the picture credits are as follows: - (t) top; (b) bottom; (l) left; (r) right; (c) centre; (AA) AA World Travel Library.

1 AA/M Jourdan; 4-18t AA/M Jourdan; 4tl AA/C Sawyer; 5 AA/C Sawyer; 6cl AA/M Jourdan; 6c AA/C Sawyer; 6cr AA/M Jourdan; 6bl AA/M Jourdan; 6bcl AA/M Jourdan; 6bcr Photodisc; 6br Photodisc; 7cl Fototeca ENIT; 7c AA/M Jourdan; 7cr AA/C Sawyer; 7bl AA/J Tims; 7bc AA/P Bennett; 7br Brand X Pics; 10tr AA/M Jourdan; 10tcr AA/M Jourdan; 10cr AA/M Jourdan; 10/11br AA/M Jourdan; 11tl AA/M Jourdan; 11tcl AA/M Jourdan; 11cl AA/C Sawyer; 13tl AA/C Sawyer; 13tcl Archivio Fotografico I.A.T. Ufficio Informazioni e Accoglienza Turistica della Provincia di Milano; 13cl Brand X Pics; 13bcl Digitalvision; 13bl Brand X Pics; 14tr David Wasserman/Brand X Pics; 14tcr AA/M Jourdan; 14cr AA/M Jourdan; 14br AA/S McBride; 15bl AA/M Jourdan; 16tr AA/M Jourdan; 16cr AA/M Jourdan; 16br AA/C Sawyer; 17tl AA/C Sawyer; 17tcl AA/C Sawyer; 17cl AA/J Holmes; 17bl AA/J Holmes; 18tr AA/M Jourdan; 18tcr Museo Nazionale della Scienza e della Tecnologia Leonardo da Vinci, Milan; 18cr AA/M Jourdan; 18br Brand X Pics; 19(i) AA/C Sawyer; 19(ii) AA/C Sawyer; 19(iii) AA/P Bennett; 19(iv) Museo Nazionale della Scienza e della Tecnologia Leonardo da Vinci, Milan; 19(v) AA/P Bennett; 20/21 AA/M Jourdan; 24tl AA/M Jourdan; 24tr AA/M Jourdan; 25tl AA/M Jourdan; 25tr AA/M Jourdan; 26t Museo Poldi Pezzoli, Milan/The Bridgeman Art Library; 27tl AA/M Jourdan; 27tr Alinari Archives/Bridgeman Reproduced with the permission of Ministero per i Beni e le Attività Culturali; 28l AA/M Jourdan; 28/29 AA/M Jourdan; 29r AA/M Jourdan; 30/31 Alinari Archives, Florence; 32-33t AA/M Jourdan; 32bl Stock Italia/Alamy; 32br AA/M Jourdan; 33b Seat Archive/Alinari Archives; 34t AA/M Jourdan; 35t AA/M Jourdan; 36t AA/M Jourdan; 37t AA/M Jourdan; 38t Digitalvision; 39t AA/C Sawyer; 40 AA/T Harris; 41 AA/M Jourdan; 44tl AA/M Jourdan; 44/45t AA/M Jourdan; 44bl AA/M Jourdan; 44bc AA/M Jourdan; 44/45b AA/M Jourdan; 45r AA/M Jourdan; 46l AA/M Jourdan; 46/47tr AA/C Sawyer; 46cr AA/M Jourdan; 46tr AA/M Jourdan; 47cl AA/M Jourdan; 47cr AA/M Jourdan; 48tl AA/M Jourdan; 48tr AA/M Jourdan; 49tl Visual&Written SL/Alamy; 49tr AA/M Jourdan; 50tl World Pictures/Alamy; 50tr Archivio Fotografico I.A.T. Ufficio Informazioni e Accoglienza Turistica della Provincia di Milano; 51t Ambrosiana, Milan/The Bridgeman Art Library; 52tl AA/C Sawyer; 52tr AA/C Sawyer; 53 Clive Tully/Alamy; 54-55t AA/M Jourdan; 54b AA/M Jourdan; 55bl AA/M Jourdan; 55br World Pictures/Alamy; 56t AA/M Jourdan; 57t AA/C Sawyer; 58t AA/M Chaplow; 58c Photodisc; 59t AA/E Meacher; 60t David Wasserman/brandxpictures; 61 AA/M Jourdan; 64 CuboImages srl/Alamy; 65tl AA/M Jourdan; 65tc AA/M Jourdan; 65tr AA/M Jourdan; 66l AA/M Jourdan; 66/67tr AA/M Jourdan; 66cr AA/M Jourdan; 67tr AA/P Bennett; 67bl AA/P Bennett; 67bc AA/M Jourdan; 67br AA/M Jourdan; 68tl AA/M Jourdan; 68tr AA/M Jourdan; 69 AA/M Jourdan; 70 World Pictures/Alamy; 71t Seat Archive/Alinari Archives; 72tl Alinari Archives Florence Reproduced with the permission of Ministero per i Beni e le Attività Culturali; 72/73tr AA/M Jourdan; 72cl AA/C Sawyer; 72cr AA/C Sawyer; 73r AA/C Sawyer; 73cl AA/C Sawyer; 74t AA/M Jourdan; 74b AA/M Jourdan; 75t AA/M Jourdan; 76t Photodisc; 77t Brand X Pics; 78t AA/A Kouprianoff; 79 AA/M Jourdan; 82/83 Seat Archive/Alinari Archives; 83tr Seat Archive/Alinari Archives; 83cr AA/M Jourdan; 84l Museo Nazionale della Scienza e della Tecnologia Leonardo da Vinci, Milan; 84/85tr Museo Nazionale della Scienza e della Tecnologia Leonardo da Vinci, Milan; 84cr Museo Nazionale della Scienza e della Tecnologia Leonardo da Vinci, Milan; 85tr Museo Nazionale della Scienza e della Tecnologia Leonardo da Vinci, Milan; 85cl Museo Nazionale della Scienza e della Tecnologia Leonardo da Vinci, Milan; 85cr Museo Nazionale della Scienza e della Tecnologia Leonardo da Vinci, Milan; 86tl AA/M Jourdan; 86bl AA/M Jourdan; 87 AA/M Jourdan; 88t AA/M Jourdan; 88bl Archivio Fotografico I.A.T. Ufficio Informazioni e Accoglienza Turistica della Provincia di Milano; 88br AA/C Sawyer; 89t AA/M Jourdan; 90t AA/M Jourdan; 91t Digitalvision; 92t AA/T Souter; 93 AA/P Bennett; 96t H P Merten/Robert Harding; 97tl AA/M Jourdan; 97tr CuboImages srl/Alamy; 98-99t AA/C Sawyer; 98b Società Trenno Ippodromi di San Siro www.trenno.it; 99b Dyana/Alamy; 100-101t AA/C Sawyer; 100bl AA/M Jourdan; 100br AA/Anna Mockford & Nick Bonetti; 101bl AA/M Jourdan; 101bc AA/C Sawyer; 101br AA/P Bennett; 102 AA/C Sawyer; 103t Digitalvision; 104t Brand X Pics; 105t AA/S McBride; 106t AA/M Jourdan; 107 AA/C Sawyer; 108-112t AA/C Sawyer; 108tr AA/Anna Mockford & Nick Bonetti; 108tcr Stockbyte Royalty Free; 108cr Royalty Free Photodisc; 108br AA/C Sawyer; 113 AA/M Jourdan; 114-125t AA/C Sawyer; 119cr AA/M Jourdan; 119br AA/C Sawyer; 120bl AA/J Edmanson; 121cr AA/M Jourdan; 122cr AA/C Sawyer; 124bl AA; 124br AA/M Jourdan; 125bl AA/P Bennett; 125br AA/C Sawyer

Every effort has been made to trace the copyright holders, and we apologise in advance for any accidental errors. We would be happy to apply the corrections in the following edition of this publication.